Jesus Decides

Jesus said to him, "I am the way, and the truth, and the life; no one comes to the Father but through Me."
John 14:6

Dear Joel and Meredith,

Knowing you and seeing God's care in the great loss you have suffered is a privilege.

Though many answers are not ours in this life... God will one day make all things right!

Meanwhile, I hope this book is some comfort.

Pastor Doug

Jesus Decides

**FROM A LIFETIME OF GRIEF
TO A MOMENT OF GRACE**

Kaye Bennett

Clark Publishing
Riverside, California

ISBN-10: 1979858292
ISBN-13: 9781979858298

This book is dedicated to the memory of:

Richard Boone Bennett

Stephanie Renee Bennett

and

Terry Carmon "Jay" Bennett, Jr.

Contents

Acknowledgments

My STORY COULD NOT HAVE been shared without having to revisit some of the worst moments and seasons of my life. It took a special friend who listened when I needed to talk and to research the things I couldn't bring myself to do. I extend a heartfelt thank you to my lifelong friend, Rita Brinner. She read my manuscript as I wrote each chapter grasshopper style, jumping from one event to another. When she said, "This is going to help so many people," it confirmed my purpose of sharing my story.

Thank you to my friend, Carolyn Evans, who encouraged me throughout my writing journey. She was the first person to read my completed manuscript. I will never forget the night she texted me at 10:00 p.m. to tell me she started reading it that day and only stopped long enough to have dinner with her husband. Part of her text read: "I believe God is going to use you to help other people."

Thank you to Cindy Clark for her friendship, encouragement, and creative instincts, for seeing me through my writing and suggesting the cover that most represented me and my story.

I knew in my heart that my manuscript wasn't the best it could be. God brought me in contact with an editor who recognized the missing pieces that I intentionally omitted and she pulled them out of me. She encouraged me to rewrite it and make each chapter as interesting as the best one. I held my breath until I received her response and was overwhelmed and validated when I did. My memoir would not be what it is without her expertise, insight, guidance and encouragement, so I extend a very special thank you to an amazing editor Trai Cartwright of Craftwrite.

Introduction

————

I was sitting at my desk one day in June of 2015. Eight months had passed since I lost my nephew and two months since I stopped drinking my way through grief. I was comparing my life to those of my friends and feeling sorry for myself.

My friends have a large family with four children and twelve grandchildren. There were three of us left in my family: my mom, brother, and me.

My friends have an airplane and could go anywhere they wanted, any time they wanted, with as many children and grandchildren as were available. I wouldn't be traveling with the children in my family again because they were gone.

My friend wrote a children's book based on one of her childhood experiences.

Wait a minute, I thought. *I can write a book, I have a story. Boy, do I have a story!*

At that very moment, I stopped feeling sorry for myself and started writing.

My story is about loss and the struggle of processing loss and grief. But more importantly, it's about knowledge. How life experiences give us knowledge in a way we never understood or knew before. The first people to realize this were Adam and Eve. They had no knowledge of good and evil, right or wrong, until they were tempted, disobeyed God and ate from the Tree of Knowledge of Good and Evil standing in the Garden of Eden.

And the eyes of them were opened and they knew that they were naked. *Genesis 3:7*

When my little brother died, my eyes were opened and I knew death and grief. I didn't want this newfound knowledge. I wanted my brother back. I was only twenty-five. Why did this happen to me and not other people my age? Someday their eyes would be opened and they would have this knowledge. No one was exempt. It comes sooner and harder for some of us.

I didn't know how to process any of it. Reconciling with everything I had to deal with took years. I don't use the word "closure" because I've heard it so many times in my life and feel it's overused when someone is grieving. How do you close feelings?

Years later, my niece was murdered by a serial killer. I already knew death and grief but now my eyes were opened and I knew murder, another unwanted knowledge. Nothing I experienced in the past could have prepared me for it. I don't have the words to describe murder other than *it's a living nightmare, a living hell.*

There's a part to murder that can only be experienced by the family members of the victim. It's the part that tears the heart out of a family. The part that you never knew existed until you know murder.

The third and last child in our family, my nephew, died from alcoholism twelve years after we lost his sister. My eyes were weary with too much knowledge, too much experience with death and grief. Dealing with his loss and the fact that both he and his sister were gone seemed unbearable at times.

Could God have intervened and prevented the tragic losses of the children in my family? Because of my faith, I knew He could have. Why didn't He? I don't know.

There were times when I was mad at God, times when I ignored Him, and times when I needed to draw close to Him again.

It was during a moment of grief for my nephew that I silently asked Jesus a question. When He answered, my eyes were opened and I knew the simplicity of His love.

I started writing with a sense of urgency, but as I wrote about the intimate details of my struggles through grief, I questioned whether I wanted to share it with anyone. Did I really want anyone to know about any of this?

At the same time, I felt a need to help other people facing similar experiences, so they would know someone else has been there and understands. I wanted them to know that regardless of what life throws at us and the unwanted knowledge of tragedy and loss we have to deal with in our lives, we can find peace.

That peace comes in knowing Jesus loves us.

CHAPTER 1
A Simple Life

I WAS RAISED WITHIN WALKING distance of a country church and it was there that I learned about God's love. I thought I would always know His love—until the day I felt He abandoned me.

Growing up, we lived in Redwood, a small rural community located in the foothills of Virginia's Blue Ridge Mountains. There was no stoplight, and it took about two seconds to drive U.S. Highway 40 through the town, passing the small post office and country store with its swinging screen front door. Most of the time a local or two would sit on the store's front porch and wave at the passing traffic.

Redwood Methodist Church was about two miles west of the post office and country store. It was a one-room country church with concrete steps leading up to its two front doors. A hymn and register board located in the front of the room displayed the attendance for the previous Sunday and the hymn numbers for the current service. Our Sunday school classes were located in different sections of the room. Most of the time during the sermon, I lay on the wooden pew with my head in my mom's lap, waiting for it to end.

My grandparent's farmhouse was about a quarter-mile west of the church. My father Terry, mother Kathryn, older brother Carmon (by twelve months and two weeks) and me lived with them. The farmhouse had an extra kitchen built on one side of it and we were able to live in our side with privacy.

Grandma Bennett favored Carmon and tolerated me. Although I was only three or four years old, I felt the difference in the way she treated me and it wasn't with kindness. One thing I inherited from my father was nose bleeds. From the time I was an infant, my nose bled almost every day and every night and not just bleeding, but pouring. One day during a nose bleed, my grandmother gave me an old rag to use and sat me on a stool next to her wood burning stove. There was a fire in the stove and the heat roasted me. I thought she was trying to kill me while she sat at the table, away from the stove, canoodling Carmon.

Grandpa Bennett was a kind man. I would sit with him in the front room of the farmhouse and listened to him sing and play hymns on his black upright piano. He sold my parents and my dad's brother, land that was part of his 110-acre farm. My dad cleared his land and built our new house across the road from Uncle Johnny's; there were two bedrooms (one for my parents and one for my brother and me), a living room, kitchen, bathroom, and a basement.

I was four when we moved into our new home. My mom hung a plate on our bedroom wall. It had a picture of a child kneeling at a bed in prayer. A child's bedtime prayer was written on the plate. Every night before my mom put us to bed and tucked us in, we knelt at the bed. My mom said a line of the prayer and we repeated it.

"Now I lay me down to sleep.
"I pray thee Lord my soul to keep.
"If I should die before I wake.
"I pray thee Lord my soul to take."

After my dad cleared the land for our house, there was a large pile of tree trunks and stumps. Carmon and I loved to crawl under them and play in a cave-like space.

"Let's fry an egg," Carmon said.

I'm sure I carried the egg because a black skillet was heavy and matches were meant for the big brother. It only took seconds before the fire started to spread and Carmon and I quickly left our cave. My dad had to call the fire department and they were able to contain it before the fire spread to the woods. When my mom tells this story, she reminds us of how upset our grandfather was, although I barely remember him being there.

My mom was a stay-at-home mom. She prepared three meals every day and my dad came home for lunch. There were hugs and kisses when he left to go back to work. On Sundays my dad took us driving. Carmon and I took turns sitting in his lap and we pretended to drive.

Two years later, when I was six, my little brother Richard was born. I loved this new baby. I wanted to be the one to rock him to sleep, to feed him, and take care of him. He slept in his crib in my mom and dad's bedroom and when he grew too big for it, he slept in the same bed with Carmon and me. But when one standard-size bed became too small for three growing children, my dad built two additional rooms onto our home that became our bedrooms. Mine also doubled as my mother's sewing room. Our original bedroom was turned into a den.

Richard became my new playmate. My mom told people I was his second mother. When he grew old enough, we spent hours playing Monopoly. He rolled the dice and I helped him count when he moved his playing piece. I managed his money and read his Chance and Community Chest cards. When he wanted to play outside in the sand box, I played with him. We built sand houses along with roads that our plastic cars and trucks drove on. Sometime we drew a circle in the sand and played marbles.

I don't know when it happened, but one day it seemed that some of the happiness was gone from our home. There were no more hugs and kisses at lunch and we didn't go driving on Sunday.

It was because of the moonshine.

When my mom told us there was a new case of moonshine in the basement (not that there were old cases of moonshine but sometimes there wasn't any), it meant that our weekends were more than likely not going to be pleasant.

My dad started drinking when he got off work on Friday and stopped when he went to bed Sunday night. When he drank, his personality changed towards my mother and we had to suffer through the argumentative outbursts. It was during one of his outbursts that I took on a new role with my little brother.

My dad was in the kitchen being verbally abusive to my mom. Richard and I were sitting in the den enduring it, waiting for it to end. Richard was always nervous during these outbursts and this time it seemed too much for him. He was trembling when he came to sit in my lap.

"Make him stop, Kaye," Richard said.

I went into the kitchen with a bravery and determination I never knew I had.

"Daddy, stop. No good will come from this," I said.

I surprised myself when I said those words but they worked. My dad stopped and left.

"Mama, are you okay?" I asked.

"Yes," she replied, but I didn't believe her.

I went back in the den and held Richard until he was calm again. I was ten years old and Richard was four when I started sheltering him during these outbursts.

Mondays through Thursdays were calmer days and we didn't have to worry about dad's drinking. He drank a beer sometimes, even let us take a sip of it, but it didn't affect him the same way the moonshine did.

Even though our weekends were stressful and sometimes chaotic, life was still simple. We lived in the country, and doors were never locked. Summer days were hot, and there was no air conditioning. At night the doors and windows were left open, leaving the screens to protect us from intruding insects. A cool breeze blew and we could hear the whistle of a train in the distance.

My dad had two large gardens, one on each side of our house. There was a strawberry patch, rows of corn, lima beans, green beans, green peas, black-eyed peas, potatoes, tomatoes, and onions. Blackberries grew wild everywhere. In the month of August, we woke up on many mornings to find a bushel of peas or beans my mom and dad picked before he went to work. Richard was too little to help, but Carmon and I spent the morning helping my mom hull them so she could freeze them the same day.

I used to think if I could have a bushel of anything that didn't require hulling, it would be a bushel of popcorn, and I'd eat all of it. Every night after dinner I popped a bowl of popcorn. The bowl was the pan my grandfather gave us to use when we picked blackberries. My brothers didn't like popcorn as much as I did, so I handed them the pan of hot popcorn and let them eat what they wanted, which wasn't very much. They soon gave the pan back to me, and I ate the rest of the popcorn while it was still warm.

My cousin Diane, Uncle Johnny's daughter, played the piano and taught me how to read music. We didn't have a piano, so I played on the one in Uncle Johnny's basement. I could play three hymns from a hymnbook, using both hands.

One of the hymns was 'What a Friend We Have in Jesus'. When I played, I not only read the music, but I also read the words and sometimes sang; a habit I would maintain for life.

What a friend we have in Jesus,
All our sins and griefs to bear!
What a privilege to carry
Everything to God in prayer!
Oh, what peace we often forfeit,
Oh, what needless pain we bear,
All because we do not carry
Everything to God in prayer!

These words say that Jesus is our friend and that we should take everything to God in prayer. I knew Jesus was God's son, so that made him like a friend. God was after all God, the main One. So, I always prayed to God. I was too young to understand what forfeiting peace, bearing sin, pain or grief really meant. I was only in the second grade and my life experiences were limited.

I begged my parents for piano lessons and started taking them when I was in the third grade. My teacher started me with the song book "Teaching Little Fingers to Play." I was a little bored. Both of my grandfathers played the piano by ear, and I guess that's why playing the piano seemed so natural to me. I was always adding things to pieces or changing things up a bit to play them the way I wanted. My mom wanted to make sure I could play hymns, so they were part of my lessons for the first several years.

I had to practice the piano for a half-hour every day after school. One day I was in the basement of Uncle Johnny's house, and my aunt was supposed to let me know when my time was up.

I always did what I was asked to do, sometimes to a fault. I sat in that basement for what seemed like an eternity. I mean, how many times in a half hour can you play two songs from "Teaching Little Fingers to Play?" I finally went upstairs and asked my aunt if time was up.

"Oh Kaye, I forgot about you," she said.

I'd been in her basement for over an hour practicing my two songs. Needless to say, I took a break from practicing for a few days. My parents eventually purchased a piano for our home, and I said goodbye to my uncle's basement.

The members of Redwood Church built a new church during the late fifties, a beautiful brick building with separate classrooms, kitchen, fellowship hall, choir room, and sanctuary. My Grandpa Bennett took part in the ground-breaking ceremony; my dad and Uncle Johnny built the cabinets for the kitchen.

The women members of Redwood Methodist Church took turns cleaning the church. My mom and aunt (the left-me-in-the-basement-for-over-an-hour aunt) volunteered together, and they were also responsible for putting flowers on each side of the altar in the sanctuary. I'm sure they picked a summer month during August because both my mom and aunt had flower gardens. Their arrangements rivaled the local florist. They took them to the church on Saturday evening so the flowers were fresh for the Sunday morning service.

While they were cleaning the church or working with the flowers, I was in the sanctuary playing hymns "How Great Thou Art," "The Church's One Foundation," "There Is a Fountain," "Bless Be the Tie," "Fairest Lord Jesus," and the list goes on. I didn't realize it then, but I look on that now as my first quiet time with God.

Miss Charlotte Seagars worked for the county in Christian Education. She was a petite lady and had a condition that is now called scoliosis, causing her to have a terrible hump on her back and stand a little bent over.

One year she asked my parents if I could accompany her to a church in the county to play the piano for the children's Christmas program. I must have been twelve or thirteen and had never played for a church service of any kind; she assured me that it would only be a few Christmas hymns. During the drive to the church, she sat on one pillow and leaned on another one to support her back. She told me about the dream she had when God said to her, "Feed My Sheep." That's when she decided to spend her life serving Him. This was the first time anyone shared their testimony with me. I knew that what she told me was important but I was naïve and remember thinking she gave up marriage and a family to serve God.

The church was a small one room and the piano was another old, out-of-tune upright, and several of the keys didn't work. There were probably only twenty people there that night, enough children to reenact the manger scene and their families. There was a sparsely-decorated Christmas tree and the children wore robes to identify their role.

As I played the Christmas hymns, I noticed a couple of the children look at me and turn their eyes away. I thought to myself, *They don't have anyone to play this piano for their church, and here I am hardly older than they are playing for their Christmas program.* This might have been their first experience of hearing this piano played. I will never forget the feeling of that evening. Miss Seagars made me feel special because she picked me. She had faith in me and believed that I could play for a Christmas program. And I felt that I was instrumental (no pun intended) in making the children's Christmas program special for them. I was so blessed to have had that experience.

I was fifteen when I played for another church service. It didn't turn out to be much of a blessing.

Carmon and I were members of the MYF—Methodist Youth Fellowship. Each year the youth were responsible for a Sunday service, and since I played the piano, they asked me to play the hymns, no prelude, offertory, doxology or postlude, just the hymns. On the Saturday before our youth Sunday, we rehearsed the service so everyone knew what they were supposed to do.

The next morning during the service, I played the introduction to the first hymn and then the congregation started singing. I tried to follow the congregation as they sang instead of setting the pace for them. Needless to say, the pace of the first hymn became slower and slower because the congregation was trying to follow my lead. I knew something was wrong but didn't know what to do. Why weren't they singing faster? I should have played the hymn at the same pace I did when I sat playing by myself, but I didn't know. The same thing happened with the second hymn, except maybe this time it grew even slower before it ended.

Did I mention there were three hymns?

The choir director, who usually played either the organ or the piano during the service, was there that day directing the choir and playing the other music. Of course she realized the problem I was having, but instead of helping me with the timing, she just sat there as I drug the congregation through two excruciatingly long hymns.

And then it happened.

Before I could play the introduction to the third hymn, the choir director got up, approached the piano, and motioned for me to remove myself from the piano bench. She sat down and played the third hymn herself.

I was humiliated. The congregation was standing, singing the hymn, and I sat on the front row pew staring straight ahead. When the service was over, I made a quick exit through the fellowship hall, never saying a word to anyone.

After lunch my mother told me that my aunt (the-left-me-in-the-basement-for-over-an-hour aunt, and now I need to give her the respect she's due: Aunt Lavon), marched to the front of the sanctuary when the service was over, removed her glasses, and gave the "evil" choir director a piece of her Christian mind. Thank you, Aunt Lavon.

But the damage had been done. Several years passed before I went back to church.

CHAPTER 2

The Band Years

——————

MY MOM STARTED WORKING AS the receptionist for the local optometrist office. Part of her schedule was noon to eight on Thursdays and Saturday until two in the afternoon. She felt comfortable because Richard and I were close and even though he was only nine or ten, he would be okay because we were at home together. We still played monopoly but had also graduated to chess. Richard almost always won. I could never get my mind wrapped around that game.

I attempted to cook meals on Thursday nights. My poor dad ate everything I tried to cook—gravy that looked and tasted like glue, boiled potatoes that were raw on the inside. He was always supportive and gave suggestions on how to improve. Richard, on the other hand, started eating canned spaghetti, soup or chili and he never stopped kidding me about the cut-up chicken I bought that turned out to be fifteen chicken wings.

I stopped taking piano lessons after my junior year in high school. Eight years of lessons was enough. I could play just about any music put in front of me. My music teacher was surprised when I quit. She thought I would pursue music in college, but I was tired of practicing and constantly being pushed to the next level.

I took Government, a required class for seniors, in summer school that year. I thought it would be a hard class and didn't want to have to deal with it as a senior. I took Typing I instead. We used manual typewriters. Only the second year students who took Typing II used electric typewriters. Once we learned the keys and started typing words and sentences, we had timing tests to determine our speed. I had the highest speed in the school, even higher than the second year students who used electric typewriters. I typed 83 words per minute on a manual typewriter.

Everyone thought I typed fast because I played the piano, but I inherited my "fast fingers" from my dad. He told me a story about when he was in the army: someone who had a desk job called in sick one day and my dad was asked to cover for him. When the supervisor realized how fast my dad could type and the amount of work he produced, he offered him the job as a permanent position, but my dad didn't want a desk job and declined.

Because of my typing speed, my guidance counselor suggested I attend National Business College in Roanoke, Virginia and study to be a secretary. I didn't know what I wanted to do after high school and didn't have any aspiration to attend a four-year college, so it sounded like a good idea. I applied for and was awarded an interest-free educational loan through my dad's work, The Lane Co., and enrolled in the Secretarial Science course. I started business school when I was seventeen, two weeks before my eighteenth birthday. Because I didn't have a car or a ride with anyone, I moved to Roanoke and lived with my Grandmother Boone.

One of my first classes was a required accounting class and I discovered my passion, working with numbers. But before I could change from Secretarial Science to Accounting, I had to prove myself to the president of the school by scoring 100% on my final exam. I took my graded exam paper into his office and only then did he allow me to transfer. It was at a time when men were accountants and women were secretaries. I became one of three girls in a thirty-plus class of accounting students.

I met Rita in college and she had a car! For the first time in my life, I experienced what it was like to do something after school besides practice the piano or do homework. We joined a sorority. I met a boy and instantly had a crush on him, but he didn't know I existed. Well, he knew I existed but not the way I wanted him to. I was in my upstairs bedroom in my grandmother's house one night, lying in bed, tossing and turning in agony because I had such a crush. I was miserable.

"God, please help me," I said.

The minute the words left my lips I felt His spirit enter the room from my right, pass through me and leave the room on my left. My agony was gone and I felt pure bliss. That's the only way I know to describe it. I thought *If heaven is like this, please let me be there now, please come back and take me with You.*

I had unintentionally called out to God and He heard me and helped me. I was surprised and a little stunned at what happened, but it felt good.

Having fun became my main objective, but it didn't benefit my accounting education. In three semesters, I went from the Dean's List to academically deficient to probation and then my parents made me move home. I was back to studying after school and back on the Dean's List the next semester.

I graduated from National Business College after two and a half continuous years with an Associate's Degree and enough accredited accounting hours to take the CPA exam. But I didn't want to be a CPA. I was twenty but looked younger and because I was nervous, soft-spoken, and didn't present myself well in an interview, I had a hard time finding a job. I interviewed with Ingersoll

Rand and was told I had more accounting education than the person I would be working for. I felt it was their way of dismissing me.

I eventually went through an agency to find a job and Travelers Insurance hired me to manually rate automobile insurance and at the same time convert the existing policies to their computer system. It wasn't accounting, but I had a job.

I needed a car. I wanted a small sports car, a Triumph TR6. My dad, Richard and I went to the Volkswagen dealership in Martinsville one Saturday morning. Richard and I rode home in my new Volkswagen instead.

Now that I had my own car, I got to do what other young adults did: drive around the town of Rocky Mount in a circle! Rocky Mount was four miles west of Redwood, and had two stoplights. There was an uptown and a downtown and you could drive around town—literally around the town in a circle. Start at the Hub Restaurant, take a left at the stoplight at the ESSO station and follow the street through "downtown." Take a left at the post office, bear to the left at the fire station and go up the hill. Take another left at the stoplight at the hospital; now you're "uptown." Follow the street, make no turns, and you'll be back at the Hub Restaurant.

On weekends, teenagers and young adults drove around town one way and if they didn't see who they were looking for, turned around and drove the other way. You couldn't miss anyone unless they were parked at Hughes Snack Bar where a car hop came to your car, took your order, and served you from a tray perched on your car window. I put sixty thousand miles on my car in two and a half years, driving back to forth to work, circling the town and occasionally driving through the parking lot at Hughes Snack Bar.

While I had been studying accounting, working at Travelers, and driving my car around Rocky Mount, Richard had been learning to play a banjo. He never showed any interest in music until he was twelve when Uncle Kelly, who never had any children of his own, gave him a banjo. Although Richard had never played one before, it only took a few instructions from one of my father's friends to show him the chords and how to pick the five-strings. Richard was gifted, self-driven, and played constantly.

My father played the guitar, and every night after dinner he took his guitar into the living room, sat on the couch next to the piano, and waited for us to come play music with him. We played bluegrass and country songs and my dad sang.

I took piano lessons for eight years and was trained to read music, not to play without it. I watched my father's hands make the chords on the guitar; he named the chord and then I knew which one to play on the piano. Over time I learned guitar chords, how to put chords together, and to play the songs without music. Some of the songs we played were "Down Yonder," "Rocky Top," and "Mountain Dew." My dad always wanted to play "The Old Rugged Cross" and "Amazing Grace."

Our older brother Carmon had been drafted into the army and was stationed at U.S. Army McCully Barracks in Wackernheim, Germany for almost seventeen months. Back then it wasn't easy to place a call to Europe, but my mother scheduled an appointment call on Christmas Eve. It was the same Christmas Richard got a brand-new Gibson five-string banjo.

It was late that night, and we all waited for the phone to ring. The phone was on the bar between the kitchen and dining room. I was sitting on a bar stool, Richard was standing next to me with his banjo ready, and my mom and dad were standing next to each other at the end of the bar. When the phone finally rang, my mom answered.

"Hello," she said, paused, and then said, "Yes, I will." She covered the receiver with her hand and told us the operator asked her to hold while she connected her with Carmon. It was only seconds before my mom said, "HELLO!" Carmon had been waiting in a telephone booth with the box of homemade Christmas cookies she had sent.

We each took turns talking to him.

"Richard got a new banjo for Christmas," my dad said.

"Can he play it?" Carmon asked. He didn't know that Richard could play the banjo and Richard was excited to surprise him.

"Yes, he can. Do you want to hear him?" my dad asked.

My dad held the telephone while Richard played a song.

Hearing Carmon's voice that night was overwhelming; it made me realize how much I missed him. It was the first time in seventeen months since we'd heard his voice. He was due to be discharged in January, only thirty days later.

Not long after, a friend of the family told my father about someone he knew whose son had a band. The boys were the same age as Richard, who was just thirteen, and thought he might be interested in playing with them. They didn't have a banjo player and it seemed a good fit, especially since by this time Richard was also playing the guitar. My mom and dad took him to Roanoke to meet them, and Richard joined "The Waylows" the same night.

The lead guitar player and singer was Bobby Smith whose father, Bob, was the manager and his mother, Lolene, was a country singer. Other members were Roger, who played the rhythm guitar; Gary, who played the base guitar; and Earl, who played the drums. They were like a family band that played mostly at Moose Lodges. Lolene's father, Ike, also played a banjo, claw hammer style (a style common to American old-time music). Ike and his wife, Lolene's mother, who was lovingly called Big Mama, sometimes went with the band and Ike joined them on stage to play a song.

One night the Waylows were playing at the Moose Lodge in Rocky Mount when my mom, dad, and I went to hear them. Bobby told me that Richard said, "You should hear my sister play the piano." He invited me to come to practice the next Wednesday, so I went with Richard.

Practice was in the finished basement of Bob and Lolene's home. There was a kitchen area with a breakfast bar and a large living space where the band set up for practice. I had a small electronic keyboard that sounded like a piano. I played two songs with Richard and spent the rest of the night trying to follow the band as they practiced. At the end of the evening, Bob announced that I was going to join the band. Everyone was welcoming; everyone except Roger, the bass player. Roger wasn't as welcoming because another band member meant less money for everyone, less money for him.

The first night I played with them in public, after just one practice session, I was so nervous that I don't think I even turned my small keyboard on or didn't have the volume high enough to be heard. I hardly knew any of the songs they were playing and only played the chords when I knew them.

Richard had to stand facing me when he played the guitar, so I could watch his hands to know which chords to play. He was on one side of the stage and I was on the other. Hopefully it wasn't too obvious. I started writing the chords to songs on index cards and had those handy but out-of-sight. I eventually bought a small notebook and kept records of the chords to all the songs we played. Over time, I learned to easily play without music.

We had to use our mom's car to haul our equipment to practice and the places we played. My parents eventually bought a baby-blue Ford Econoline panel van for Richard. He put a partition in the van and stored our equipment behind it. He put paneling on the front of the partition and on the sides of the van and carpet on the floor and ceiling. Richard took good care of our equipment; it always looked like new, even though it had to be unloaded and loaded three times a week.

We eventually upgraded our instruments. Our parents bought Richard a slightly-used Gibson electric guitar and amplifier. I replaced the tiny keyboard with an electric piano and also bought a new string synthesizer. Richard found a Hammond Porta B organ with a Leslie amplifier, and one night we surprised the rest of the band members when we brought it to practice. I thought it was a surprise but no one seemed at all shocked.

I also changed jobs and traded my car. After having been at Travelers Insurance for two and a half years, I went to work for Fleetwood Homes, a manufacturer of mobile homes, travel trailers, and motor homes. I worked as the plant accountant in their mobile home plant in Rocky Mount. I traded my Volkswagen for the Triumph TR6 I had always wanted. Richard drove it in the homecoming parade that year, top down, with one of the girls on the homecoming court sitting on the back. I drove his van and parked in a spot where I could get his picture while he drove "around" the town in the parade.

Richard wanted a steel guitar, but the problem was that he didn't have the money to buy one. He was sixteen years old, and his only income was from playing in the band. The steel guitar he wanted was a Marlin, which was handmade in Eden, North Carolina, and cost five hundred dollars. He asked my parents for the money, but they hadn't responded yet, so we decided to go to the bank and borrow the money. I was twenty-three and co-signed for Richard. On Saturday we went to Eden, and he ordered a single neck steel guitar. He had also learned to play the trumpet in school, so now he was playing the banjo, guitar, steel guitar, and trumpet.

The Waylows became popular because we could play a variety of music—country, bluegrass, and rock. Other than Moose Lodges, venues included country clubs or the ballroom of Hotel Roanoke for private parties, especially during Christmas and on New Year's Eve.

Richard and Bobby became good friends and were always kidding around on stage. One time we were at a Moose Lodge, and were waiting for Bobby to announce our next song. It was a country song called "Rolling in My Sweet Baby's Arms."

"We're going to play a little song for you now called 'Rolling in My Sweet Baby's Legs,'" Bobby announced.

We all looked at each other in surprise and just started laughing. Another time we were playing "Gitarzan" by Ray Stephens. It's a funny song, and somewhere in the lyrics it mentions a monkey. At that point in the song, Richard made monkey sounds. One night he hid a banana in his jacket, and when it was time for him to make the monkey noises, Bobby noticed that Richard wasn't doing his part. When he looked over, Richard was peeling the banana, getting ready to take a bite. Bobby stopped singing and started laughing right into the microphone.

Bobby and Lolene sang almost all of the songs. Richard and I had never sung, but Bobby encouraged us to try. Singing came naturally for Bobby. I wanted to sing but knew I didn't have a strong voice. I gave it a try anyway. For several weeks, I practiced "Let Me Be There" by Olivia Newton-John.

The night came when I was going to sing for the first time. We were into our third hour and had one more song to play before we took our break when Bobby announced my song. He not only announced it but also told everyone that I'd never sang before, had been practicing for weeks, and was going to sing tonight for the first time.

"She's my sister, she's single, and we need the room at home!" Richard added to Bobby's announcement.

As I made my way from behind the organ to the front of the stage and took the microphone, I broke out in a cold sweat. I appreciated Bobby's and Richard's comments because they were supportive and excited for me, and Richard was probably a little proud. It also helped fill in the time it took me to get to the microphone; I felt like I was walking in slow motion. Hardly anyone danced. Most people either sat at their tables or stood on the dance floor and merely watched and listened while I sang. When I finished, I was trembling, but I made it through. I felt comfortable that it sounded okay, and everyone was supportive with their applause. Then we took a break; I seriously needed one at that point.

Richard was well-known for his banjo playing. He and two of his high school friends also played music together. One friend played a mandolin and the other a standup bass. One night, they played in a show at Franklin County High School. Richard led the way when they walked on the stage, pushed his banjo high above his head and when the audience saw him, they cheered. I walked down one of the isles and got close to the stage so I could take their picture. That was my little brother on the stage that everyone loved; I was so proud of him.

Richard was easy going; I never heard him raise his voice in anger to anyone. He was affectionate and many times I saw him standing at the kitchen counter next to our mom with his arm around her shoulders, giving her a hug. He loved life, family, music and enjoyed sharing it with other people. He was the kind of little brother who woke me up at midnight with two bowls of home-made peach ice cream our mom had made, one for me and one for him. He wanted to tell me about the concert he had been to while we ate our ice cream.

This was also about the time I decided that I wanted to go back to church. On Saturday nights we came home from playing and got back to Rocky Mount anywhere from two-thirty to three in the morning. My mom woke me up after I had only slept for a few hours so I could go to church with her. After Sunday lunch, I slept again.

At one point Mattie Johnson, a member of the church, asked me if I would consider playing for the church service. They already had someone playing the piano, so I agreed to play the organ. Sometimes I was half-asleep when I played on Sunday morning, but it felt good to be back at church and be part of the service, this time without the "evil" choir director.

Now that I had an income, I had to decide on my giving. It seemed only natural to me that I should tithe, return ten percent to God. I actually gave more than a tithe. I grew up watching my mother prepare her offering envelope every Sunday morning before we left for church and place it in the collection plate during the service. I don't know if she tithed or what the amount of her check was, but she never missed a Sunday. If, for any reason, she missed church altogether, she placed two envelopes in the offering plate the next Sunday. My mother had been an excellent example of faithfulness. Because I played the piano during the service, I prepared my check and envelope and asked my mother to put it in the offering plate for me.

I bought a new Bible, *The Way: The Living Bible*, and was randomly reading it when God communicated with me in a way I had never experienced before. It was one of those moments, the first time for me, when God's word became more than words on a page and more than part of a story. They became larger than life. The verses were from the book of Job.

"Where were you when I laid the foundations of the earth? Tell me, if you know so much. Do you know how its dimensions were determined, and who did the surveying? What supports its foundations, and who laid its cornerstone, as the morning stars sang together and all the angels shouted for joy?" *Job 38:4–7.*

I was overwhelmed and humbled at the same time. I felt that we take so much for granted every day. Do we stop to think there is also a cornerstone that God set in place somewhere inside this planet we live on? He did the surveying and determined the dimensions. He determined north, south, east, and west.

One night I was reading *Ecclesiastes* and came upon the "time for everything" verses: a time to be born, a time to die, a time to plant, a time to harvest, and so on. I immediately went into Richard's bedroom and saw that he was also reading his Bible. I was excited to tell him what I'd discovered.

"Look, this sounds like the Simon and Garfunkel song," I said.

"Of course it is," he replied. "Where do you think they got the words?"

Now that I was attending church again and felt comfortable being involved, I wanted to sing. Unlike the first time I sang with the band when I was nervous, this time I was excited and confident. I chose "One Day at a Time," a popular contemporary song.

I could never have known it then, but there would be many times in my lifetime when I would struggle to live *one day at a time.*

CHAPTER 3

Memorial Day 1975

———

RICHARD AND I HAD BEEN playing in the band for five years. When we started playing, we played one night each weekend, but as the band became more popular, we were constantly booked. Bob Smith, our manager, had purposely not booked Memorial Day weekend in 1975. We had the entire week off, no practice during the week and no performances on the weekend.

You would think because we spent so much time together, the band members would make separate plans for the weekend. But because we were friends, we planned to go to a concert on Friday night and see The Eagles and Linda Ronstadt at the Roanoke Civic Center. I made plans to then go to Myrtle Beach, South Carolina for two days with a friend and her mother. We'd planned to leave late Saturday night, drive all night, and arrive at the beach on Sunday morning. That way we didn't have to pay for a hotel for Saturday night.

On Saturday night of that Memorial Day weekend, my mom prepared the meal. All of us, including my dad, were there. Carmon, his wife Mollie, their baby Jay, who was almost thirteen months old, were also there for dinner. We had an enjoyable time together, and it truly felt like a family dinner. It hadn't always been the case because of my dad's drinking, so it was like a gift from

God that our family had such a good time that night. We talked, laughed, and shared stories.

"I'm going to end up in Nashville someday and you will still be in Rocky Mount doing accounting," Richard teased me.

We laughed about it. He was so talented that he probably would end up in Nashville and be very successful.

After dinner, I went into the den and sat in my dad's leather chair. A feeling of dread came over me. Suddenly, I didn't want to go to the beach with my friend and her mother. Richard was going to take me to Roanoke to meet them for the Myrtle Beach trip. We decided to take my car and left.

We met my friend in a shopping center parking lot. Richard told me to be sure to call when I got to the beach, so they would know I arrived safely. I told him to be careful driving home. I even repeated it. I got in the back seat of my friend's car. As we left the parking lot, Richard was behind us; I turned around twice to wave to him.

We stayed at my friend's home until one in the morning, and then we left. As we drove to the beach, we headed back toward Rocky Mount and passed through Boones Mill, a small town with one stoplight on Route 220. When we came to the top of the hill and were able to see the next hill, it was lit up like a Christmas tree. There was a fire truck, an ambulance, maybe two, and several other vehicles parked alongside the road. When we passed by, an accident had happened. We couldn't see the vehicle that wrecked, but there was a dead dog in the road. I commented that living in a small town it was scary to see accidents because it might be someone you know.

We continued on to Myrtle Beach and arrived sometime before noon. The rooms weren't ready for us to check into, so we waited in the lobby of the hotel. I became anxious and thought I should call home and let my family know I arrived safely. I tried two different pay phones on the street, neither of which worked. I made a collect call home using a pay phone near the hotel lobby. When my aunt answered, I sensed something was wrong.

"Aunt Lavon?" I questioned.

She told me I needed to come home. When I asked why, she repeated for me to come home. I made her tell me why.

"Richard is gone," she said.

"What do you mean, he's gone?" I asked.

"He wrecked on his way home last night and died."

I guess I started yelling and crying or something because my friend and her mother came to me right away. I had dropped the telephone and the receiver was hanging in midair. I told them what happened. I felt as if I was moving in slow motion as we made our way to the hotel lounge for privacy.

Richard was gone! Richard was dead! I had heard those words! How could this possibly be happening? I felt confused. Was this real? I didn't know what I was supposed to say or do. I sat in a chair in the lounge and listened to my friend and her mother call to find a flight for me to return home. I had never flown before. Was I supposed to be anxious about flying? Was I supposed to be excited? Then I thought that if I flew home I wouldn't be able to tell Richard about it. He wouldn't be there to pick me up. Nothing seemed right. I didn't know what I was supposed to feel, what I was supposed to be doing or saying.

After a few minutes of stunned confusion, I gave way to crying and then sobs.

The ride back was long and arduous. I napped, cried, and endured the quiet times when no one spoke. It was stressful for everyone in the car. I reflected on the events of the past few hours and realized that God hadn't wanted me to be by myself on the street using a pay phone when I learned of my brother's death. A simple gift in the midst of the nightmare I suddenly found myself in.

When we turned from the highway onto the road that led to our home, there were cars everywhere. Richard's van was parked behind the house in the grass. It was raining hard and because of all of the cars we couldn't get close. I got out and ran to the house and up the steps to the back door. Our home was full of relatives, and I surprised everyone when I appeared. I went to both my mom and dad for comfort, but instead I saw a state of extreme shock and grief for the first time in my life.

They told me what happened after Richard dropped me off. He tried to find Bobby, his best friend and our band leader, but ended up at the home of another friend who had a band. It was after midnight when he drove my car through Boones Mill on his way back to Rocky Mount. A friend of Richards had pulled onto the highway behind him.

As they were going up the hill, two dogs ran out in front of Richard. He swerved to miss them, but there wasn't enough room on the edge of the road and my car went off the road and plowed into the side of the mountain. Richard's friend in the car behind him immediately went back to the rescue squad building in Boones Mill for help, but Richard had been killed instantly. That was the accident we had driven by the night before.

Richard died on Sunday May 25, 1975, Memorial Day. He was nineteen years old.

On Monday morning, the funeral director asked for clothes for Richard. My mom cried as she selected one of the tuxedos he had worn in the band. We went to the funeral home Monday afternoon, the day of the visitation, for the family viewing. We sat in one of the rooms while the funeral director spoke with us. He advised that we not view Richard's body because of the injuries.

"I would like to see my son," my mom quietly said.

"If it were my son, I wouldn't want his mother to see him like this," the funeral director replied.

My mom was reduced to sobs. I couldn't hold back the deep guttural cry that escaped from me. I walked out of the room, out of the funeral home to the front of the building. Carmon followed me.

"Richard was thrown through the windshield onto the motor and most of the bones in his body were broken," Carmon said.

I couldn't say anything; I just cried. My heart hurt. We had to go back in because my mom and dad were waiting for us to view the closed casket together.

The baby I loved from the minute my parents brought him home from the hospital, the little boy who learned to count when we played Monopoly, my little brother who I sheltered from the argumentative outbursts and mothered his entire life, my best friend, was lying in that casket. I couldn't see him and I couldn't say goodbye to him.

"Don't cry, Kaye," my mom said. "If it had been you, Richard wouldn't have been able to deal with it."

How was I supposed to deal with it?

We spent the next few days going through the motions of a funeral; the visitation lasted for hours. Richard and I had been at the same funeral home only six months earlier when a teenage cousin died in a motorcycle accident. When we got out of the car, I told Richard that if anything ever happened to him or Carmon, I didn't know what I would do.

"There's nothing you can do," he said. "What's done is done."

He had been right. There was nothing to do but try and get through it.

The funeral procession drove through the town of Rocky Mount on the way to Redwood Methodist Church. I saw people walking, laughing, and talking and couldn't believe they were going on with their lives as if nothing had happened, while our lives had been shattered.

The sanctuary was packed with more people also standing outside. The service itself was short. I helped my mom prepare it and neither of us felt we could sit through anything too long. We included the "Time for Everything" verses from Ecclesiastes, the ones I had shared with Richard.

As the funeral procession made its way to the cemetery, police were along the route controlling the traffic. They saluted us, and it seemed appropriate, to be acknowledging our loss. When the graveside service was over, family and friends came to our home for a meal. This was so strange to me. How could they enjoy a meal after what we'd just experienced? Again, almost everyone was talking, laughing, and acting as if nothing had happened.

My cousin Linda was a medical secretary, and the doctor she worked for provided us with a prescription for Valium. I took two the day of the funeral. The day's events over, the Valium relaxed me to the point that I almost fell asleep sitting in my chair. I should say to the point that I almost fell out of the chair onto the floor. The best part about taking the pills was that I slept well, no tossing or turning, no dreams, just sleep.

Richard's bedroom and mine shared a common wall. I was so used to hearing him in his room, almost always playing the guitar. One night he was playing a song on his stereo and had his headphones on. He was trying to learn a song and I heard him practice for what seemed like hours. I used to complain that I couldn't sleep because of his practicing, but now wished I could hear it.

Several weeks after Richard's funeral, my cousin and I stopped by Richard's grave to see if the marker had been installed. When I saw my little brother's name on a gravestone, I felt as if a knife had been thrust into me. Everything had been such a blur—one day he was here; the next he was gone. It didn't seem real. One day he would come home and ask what all the fuss had been about. Seeing his name on the marker was sobering and made his death convincingly real.

Jay was fifteen months old then. He knew that Richard was somewhere in the cemetery but of course he didn't understand what was going on. Whenever we drove by the cemetery and saw that they were preparing a grave, Jay saw the equipment and said, "Richard's backhoe."

Chimes were placed in the church in memory of Richard that year. Carmon and I participated in the dedication during the Sunday service; he spoke and I played the organ along with the chimes. I played "Morning Has Broken," a hymn originally written in 1931 but made famous in 1971 by Cat Stevens, a pop musician and folk singer. The feel of the song suited Richard's easy-going personality. I chose it because he had been trying to learn to sing it.

As I played the organ that day, my foot slipped on the volume pedal and the music went from normal to extremely loud. Everyone looked at me, worried, as if something had happened to me. I started laughing. I think Richard would have laughed, too.

CHAPTER 4

A Rough Road

———

I WAS TWENTY-FIVE YEARS OLD when life slapped me in the face and said, "Wake up; this is reality!" When Richard died, I not only lost my little brother but I also lost my best friend. I was in a state of shock but didn't know I was in shock. Trying to deal with what happened was incredibly hard. He died on a Sunday, the funeral was two days later on Tuesday, and I had to play in the band on Friday and Saturday night. The band had commitments and we had to keep them.

The first night playing, I could hear Richard play; I could see him walk across the room. It was so strange that he wasn't with us. All I could do was sit behind the organ and play. I couldn't sing my one song. Every time I made eye contact with someone on the dance floor, I imagined they were thinking, "The boy who died, that's his sister."

Bobby, somehow lead us through the night. I can only imagine how hard it must have been for him. He'd lost his grandfather *and* best friend within a matter of days. They both played the banjo, and now Bobby had to in their stead.

Bobby had to skirt around the songs that featured Richard. It was awkward for all of us; there were moments we just looked at each other, wondering what to do next. Those feelings of hearing him play and imagining him walking across the room stayed with me, especially when we played at a venue for the first time without him.

My car was totaled in the wreck, and I was driving Richard's van now. It was well over a year before I could bring myself to get another car. While I was driving his van, I passed people who knew me, but no one waved or acknowledged me. I didn't understand—I wasn't the one who died. Why, all of a sudden, was I invisible?

One day I was shopping and ran into someone who said, "I saw you driving Richard's van the other day. How is he doing?" That caught me off guard. When I told him that Richard died, he was shocked. He gave his condolences, made a quick excuse, and left me standing by myself. In the instant it took him to leave, I wondered, *What just happened?*

One Wednesday night I left band practice and was driving back to Rocky Mount. A German shepherd ran out in front of me. I gripped the steering wheel and forced myself not to react. I killed the dog and started crying. If Richard had not tried to save an animal, he would still be with us. If he had been driving his van that night instead of my car, things may have turned out different. Maybe he wouldn't have tried to miss the dog.

I continued to play in the band for a few months. Either Mollie or my cousin Linda went with me those first weeks after he died. But I knew that couldn't go on forever because Mollie had a husband, my brother, and a child, Jay, to take care of, and Linda had a life she needed to lead. I finally got to the point where I was okay to go alone, but it was still hard to be out by myself that late at night. Sometimes I was so tired driving home in the early morning hours that I saw people in telephone booths who weren't really there.

One night I was driving through Boones Mill on my way home from playing. It was about two-thirty in the morning and a passenger van full of guys passed by me and slowed down. They pulled in front of me and slowed down even more. I was unsure and a little afraid of what might happen next. When Richard was alive, the only time I drove his van was just one or two times when he was sick. He lay in the back of the van while I drove home. During those times, anyone who saw me couldn't have known that I wasn't alone. But this time, I was alone and missed the comforting feeling of Richard being there. The next thing I saw that night was two bare butts, one black and one white, in each window of the back of the van in front of me. I turned my lights off.

Thankfully they let me pass and the distance between us increased. I was relieved once I realized nothing else was going to happen. They were just amusing themselves. Then I laughed.

I decided I didn't want to play in the band any longer. It was too much without Richard, and I didn't enjoy it anymore. I needed to move on. I sat on the couch in the den, trying to get myself to go to Bob and Lolene's and tell them. I finally decided to do it, but before I left, I said out loud, "God, if you don't want me to do this, please stop me."

I was taking my mother's car, so I told her I was leaving and went outside. As I started to pull the door open, it shut on my thumb. My thumb was mashed at the base of the nail, the skin broken and bleeding.

"Okay, God, I'm not going," I said.

To this day, that thumbnail still looks a little different.

I didn't have anyone to talk to about Richard's passing. All of us in the band were in shock, and we didn't talk about Richard much. We kept on playing, everyone dealing with his death in their own way. I had never talked to my mom and dad about anything, so having them help me through this was not going to happen. They had enough to deal with on their own: they had lost their youngest child, their baby, and were suffering. I felt like a stepchild because I felt so ignored. I needed help, but so did they.

Christmas was only a few months away, and I dreaded it. How could we get through Christmas without Richard? In November my dad became sick with what we thought was the flu. Several days went by, and he got worse. My mom took him to the doctor and he was admitted to Franklin Memorial Hospital with viral pneumonia. I was working, playing in the band and expected my dad to get well and be home soon. I visited him often but didn't realize how serious his condition was until about a week later when he was transferred to the intensive care unit in Roanoke Memorial Hospital. Worrying about my dad's health replaced my dread of Christmas without Richard.

I was at work the day before Christmas Eve when my grandmother called. My mom couldn't make a long distance call from the hospital so she called my grandmother, who lived in Roanoke and asked her to call me.

"I just talked to your mom. She said the doctors told her that your dad isn't going to make it, and you and Carmon should get to the hospital as soon as you can," my grandmother said.

I called Carmon and he picked me up. He drove the twenty-five miles to Roanoke with the emergency flashers on. He was speeding to the point of reckless driving.

"What are we going to do if you get pulled over for speeding?" I asked.

"Ask them to escort us to the hospital," he said.

That was the extent of our conversation during the drive.

We walked into the small ICU waiting room. My mom was by herself, sitting in a chair in the corner, crying and withdrawn.

"I told the doctors that your dad was a heavy drinker in case they needed to do anything to help him because of it," she said.

Only two people at a time were allowed to visit the patients in intensive care and only for ten minutes at the designated times. My mom and I went in together and I was shocked when I saw my dad. I hadn't seen him in three days because of my work and band commitments. He had lost a lot of weight and was very thin. He was hooked up to oxygen and he appeared to be asleep. When we went back into the waiting room, I started crying, walked over to the window, rested my forehead on the window pane and raised my hand up to the glass. I wanted to reach out to God for help. Surely He wouldn't take my dad and Richard in the same year. Surely we wouldn't lose my dad at Christmas. It had only been seven months, almost to the day, that we lost Richard.

"He's so sick," I said, through tears.

By that time, several other relatives had arrived. My cousin Patricia helped me to a chair. We sat in vigil that night, afraid of any news. Thankfully, my dad did not pass like the doctors predicted, but they told us that he came within the width of his little fingernail of dying. We spent Christmas Eve and Christmas Day in the hospital, grateful and relieved that my father was alive and would recover.

Christmas had come and gone, and Richard's name had rarely been mentioned. My dad came home from the hospital in late January, life went on, and still we hardly talked about Richard. Somehow it just seemed easier for everyone.

My grief went deep inside.

I quit playing in the band but didn't remember when I told them or how I told them. I didn't remember anything about it, only that I didn't play anymore. My new routine was work and church, not much more than that. Although I had a couple of friends I visited once in a while, if I wanted to go to a movie, I went by myself.

I experienced moments when I wanted to talk to Richard. Something happened to remind me of him or something came up that I wanted to talk to him about, and I cried and grieved. There were a couple of times when I thought I could feel his presence. Once when I was cleaning the inside of the van I couldn't get the curtain rod back in place. All I had to do was put it back in the hole it came out of. It seemed as though something was blocking it and then I felt Richard's presence. I thought, *Is he playing games with me?* I decided he was because in the next moment the rod went easily into place. Those times were surreal but made me realize his absence even more. It was like he wanted to be with me. I wanted him to be with us again, too.

Our best distraction and source of comfort was Jay. He was a toddler, and we all poured our love into him. Carmon, Mollie, and Jay had dinner with us on Wednesday nights and lunch every Sunday after church. Jay was always the center of our attention; he helped fill the void of Richard's absence and was the bright spot in our lives. We finally reached a level of reasonable daily functioning, of moving forward and learning to live without Richard.

It had been a little over a year since we lost Richard and I was in bed one Saturday morning when the phone rang. The call was from my dad's work. He was the maintenance supervisor for the Lane Company, a furniture manufacturer. There had been an accident, and he had been burned, a steam and acid burn.

"Kaye, it's bad," his friend said.

I called my mom at work and then Carmon. We met at the hospital emergency entrance. On weekends, the local doctors were on call for the emergency room. The doctor on call would not come to the hospital because he was busy with the patients in his office, so they had to put my dad back in the ambulance and take him to the doctor's office. When we saw him, he was on a gurney in the hall, waiting to be transported twenty-five miles to Roanoke Memorial Hospital. He had third-degree burns on the right side of his body, back, arm, and head. The doctor there had given him a shot for pain.

When Carmon and I saw my dad partially covered with only a sheet, his body scorched, his skin curled and barely hanging on his arm, we became angry with the doctor.

"We're going to sue the doctor for not coming to the hospital," Carmon said and I agreed.

"No, we're not going to sue anybody," my dad said. It must have been the shot for pain that allowed my dad to lay on the gurney patiently waiting for an ambulance and calmly correct his two adult children.

It was several weeks and several skin grafts later before he was released. I came home for lunch one day and there was my dad sitting at the bar between the kitchen and dining room. I had expected him later in the afternoon but he had been released early. We ate lunch together for the first time in almost two months.

"I saw the flat tire in the garage basement. Why didn't you tell me about it?" Dad asked.

"I did tell you. It was when you were still in isolation at Roanoke Memorial." I said.

He had forgotten. I had it fixed myself.

Even though I'd had a flat tire and a couple of other minor problems with the van, when I was driving it, I was in a comfort zone. I needed that comfort zone because my brother died when he was driving my car. I felt that I didn't deserve to own a nice car again. I had received the check from the insurance company, reimbursing me for my totaled car, but I didn't want it. I wanted my brother back. It was one of those life lesson moments for me when money and material things were put into a different perspective.

Eventually I did buy a used Ford Bronco. It wasn't a car, it wasn't nice; in fact, it was dirty. It was very dirty. It belonged to a farmer who had only used it on his farm. I cleaned it, cleaned it again, installed carpet, had the wheel wells cut out, installed white fender flares, and replaced the regular tires with larger, wider ones mounted on new wheels. I put a white tire cover on the spare tire mounted on the back.

The Bronco looked good, but every time I drove it I could see the gas hand move as the tank drained. The Bronco had to go. I sold it at my asking price to the first person who was interested in buying it. He got in the Bronco to leave, turned the key, and the battery was dead. What were the chances?

I had taken two steps forward and one backward. I bought a vehicle that I really didn't like. I played around with it, fixed it up, and then got rid of it. I went back to my comfort zone, driving Richard's van.

The year passed, and we prepared for another Christmas. It was as if nothing had ever happened. We went to my grandmother's on Christmas Eve, back to my parents for our Christmas gift exchange, and then went to Carmon's on Christmas morning to see what Santa had brought for Jay. My grandmother, my mother's sisters and their husbands, plus Carmon, Mollie, and Jay all came to our house for dinner Christmas night. I sat in the living room watching everyone: it looked like Christmas as usual. Was I the only one who missed Richard? Was I the only one who noticed he wasn't there? It was good to see everyone back to what seemed normal, especially my mom and dad, but it still hurt that no one ever mentioned his name.

That winter was a rough one as far as weather was concerned; there was a lot of snow and ice. Since I was no longer playing in the band, my dad had unloaded my equipment and stored it in the garage. Without the equipment, there was nothing to weigh the van down and driving it in those conditions was unsafe. I relented and accepted that it was time for me to get a car.

This time I bought a used Volvo; it was old, it was sort of clean, it was green (a green car?) and it used almost as much oil as it did gas. One thing I knew for sure about that car: the oil light was bright red, and I would see it often. I had taken two more steps forward in the process of owning a nice car again, and this time I kept moving forward.

Now that I'd had two used vehicles that were high mainte-nance, I decided it was time to own a decent car. I found one that was slightly used but looked like new, a blue Datsun 280Z. I brought it home and didn't drive the van or the Volvo again.

I had taken two more steps forward and none backward. Getting to the point of owning a nice car had been part of my grieving process. Now that was behind me. I was moving on.

CHAPTER 5

The Problem with Grief

———

Two times during the years that I worked at Fleetwood Homes in Rocky Mount, I had a new general manager, a new boss. Fleetwood Home's system was structured so office employees were only eligible for evaluations and raises on their anniversaries with the company. I processed the payroll and knew everyone's anniversary date and rate of pay. Other people received evaluations that included raises, but the new general manager would not evaluate me on my fifth anniversary because he "hadn't worked with me long enough." I started looking for another job.

I must have been doing something right because after I found a job and gave a two-week notice, Fleetwood's corporate office in Riverside, California flew me there to be interviewed by several people to work in the Information Technology (computer) department as support for the plants. My general manager said, "They're not going to let you go because you've done such a good job." Hello! If you had evaluated me and told me that on my anniversary, I wouldn't have looked for another job.

Life seemed good again, but now my family had another major life event to deal with: mine. It was a hard decision to make, but I told my family I was moving to California. I knew it hurt them, but I had to have a life and would probably never have this kind of opportunity again. About a month later in August, one month before my twenty-eighth birthday, I put my clothes and whatever else I could get into the back of my 280Z and, with the help of my cousin Linda, drove to California.

We made a vacation of it, stopping in Nashville, visiting Graceland in Memphis, the Grand Canyon, and then we took a small detour to spend the night in Las Vegas. I was having an adventure right up until we arrived in Riverside, and then it hit me that I wasn't going home. Because I was so homesick, I think everyone gave me about two weeks max and then figured I'd be on my way back to Virginia. But I stuck it out.

To my knowledge, I was the first woman in the Fleetwood organization to be transferred within the company. With this new job, I got to travel and discovered that I loved it. For someone who'd hardly been away from home, every trip was exciting.

My job was to train people to use the computer, but because I knew accounting, they also asked me to work on other projects. I had only been in California for a month when I was sent to Sunnyside, Washington. I left on Monday and was supposed to be back on Friday, but I ended up staying three-and-a-half weeks. Needless to say, I grew tired of wearing the same clothes, but I had a lot of memorable experiences while I was there.

One weekend I drove a rental car through the mountains, getting as close to Mt. Rainier as I could. I sat for a couple of hours soaking up the breathtaking view. This mountain was nothing like the Blue Ridge Mountains of Virginia. It was majestic, snow-capped, and regal, mounted against a clear blue sky. A nice guy who worked at the plant took me to the Washington State Fair. He played the games and won several stuffed animals; one was a large bulldog named Butch. Another weekend we went sailing on the Columbia River.

The operations manager also invited the plant accountant and me to go horseback riding on his ranch. I was a little apprehensive. The only horse I had ever been on was an old one that ambled along the trail when our church youth group went to Fairy Stone State Park in Stuart, Virginia. But ride the horse I did. I was surprised to discover that the lower elevations in Washington State were barren. It reminded me of prairies. When we were riding that day, I felt God's presence. He was with me, out there on the prairie. I felt comforted, loved and not alone.

I had been back in Riverside for two weeks and then I was sent to Indiana. When I finished my work there, I took advantage of being close to home and went to Virginia for the weekend. I brought Butch with me for Jay. The flight attendants teased me and said that he needed his own seat because he was so big. When I arrived in Roanoke, my mom, Dad, Carmon, Mollie, and Jay were there to greet me. I hugged Jay first and gave him Butch. At first he wasn't too sure about that stuffed animal, but eventually warmed up to him. Then I hugged everyone else. My dad was funny because he'd never been an affectionate father; hugging him was like hugging a board. Over time he got used to it, and I could tell that he expected the hug, although he never initiated it.

Other places I traveled were Omaha, Nebraska, Benton Harbor, Michigan, and Boulder, Colorado. I met so many nice people who went out of their way to take care of me. Each time I was sent somewhere, if I was close to Virginia or if my trip coupled with a holiday, I always went home to visit and brought Jay a t-shirt from where I'd been.

Even though I was based out of California, I didn't spend much time working there. As a result, I didn't have time to develop friendships outside of work. The only people I knew were the ones

I worked with. At times I tried to tell them about Richard and what happened two or three years earlier, but no one was interested.

One of the first things I bought after moving to California was a piano. One night my roommate, also a co-worker, and I entertained other co-workers who knew my story. They wanted to hear me play, so I played one of the songs Richard, my dad and I used to play. They had never heard the song. I started crying when I explained how the three of us played music.

"Why are you crying?" a friend asked.

"Sometimes things just seem fresh again." I said.

"I've never seen anyone grieve the way you do over your brother."

I realize now that they probably had never heard anyone grieve; they probably hadn't experienced grief at all. How many people have, at the age of twenty-five, lost their little brother? Regardless of whom I talked to, I got the same reaction. They were good friends but not the kind who took the time to truly listen and try to understand.

Carmon and Mollie had their second child, a daughter named Stephanie. I went home two weeks after she was born and Jay met me at the front door.

"Don't go in there to see her. She's just sleeping," he said. "Come play with me."

Jay was five years old when he became a big brother.

Of course I went in to see my new niece and discovered that she looked like me, for a few days anyway. A day or so later, Carmon, Mollie, Jay, and baby Stephanie came to my mom and dad's house. She was asleep in a baby carrier on the dining room table. I was alone in the room with her, and I rubbed my index finger on her arm and said, "Hey, new baby." She smiled. What a beautiful smile she had.

After living in California for two and a half years, the economy turned downward, business was affected, and my traveling was eliminated. Since I hadn't been there long enough to develop a network of friends and I wouldn't be able to travel, I decided to move back to Virginia to my old job.

Before I left California, my coworkers decided I needed to do some of the things I'd not yet done. One Saturday we went to the San Diego Zoo where I absolutely fell in love with giraffes. What beautiful and graceful animals they are! They took me to a Dodgers baseball game. We also went to a Bee Gees concert at Dodgers stadium. It was packed with about fifty thousand people. The field was thick with people bouncing beach balls and using blankets to throw people into the air as if they were on a trampoline.

I sat in a seat amid thousands of people, but the seat next to me was empty. Before the concert began, I asked to borrow binoculars from someone sitting near me so I could see the "stars" who were seated in the VIP section. Suddenly, I felt Richard's presence in the seat next to me. The feeling was so strong that I had to immediately take the binoculars from my eyes and look at the seat. It was still empty.

Carmon flew to California to help me drive home. We left Riverside one Friday afternoon and drove to Las Vegas since Carmon had never been there. Saturday morning at five a.m. we headed east, stopped in Amarillo, Texas to sleep for a few hours, and then continued on to Virginia. This was the most time we had ever spent together. Even though we were close in age, only thirteen months apart, Carmon and I had never had a close relationship. One thing I learned about him that weekend was how much he loved his children. All he talked about during our trip across the country was Jay and Stephanie.

Forty-eight hours after we left Las Vegas, we pulled into my parent's driveway. I was home again. I quickly got back into the swing of things, working, attending church, and spending lots of time with my niece and nephew.

Jay was in the first grade and rode on the console between the seats of my Datsun 280Z.

"Katie, I have a problem and I need to talk to you about it," he said one day when we were riding in my car.

"What is it?" I asked.

"At school, I finish my school work first and the teacher won't let me go outside and play. I have to wait for everybody else to finish. I don't think it's fair." Jay said.

"Well, that's one of the hard parts of school, isn't it? It seems like you're being punished because you finish first. But you still have to mind the teacher," I said.

"How come you know the answers to all the questions I ask you?"

"Well, it's because I'm a little older than you are and right now you ask me easy questions. Someday when you're older, I might not have all the answers to your questions."

Sometimes when he was riding with me, we played word games. I mixed up the letters and he would guess it. He never missed one. Even at a young age, it was evident how smart he was.

On Sunday afternoons, after lunch, we went to the movies if there was a kid appropriate one. One Sunday I was at the counter buying drinks and popcorn. My arms were full with our jackets, my purse, the drinks, and a bucket of popcorn. As I tried to maneuver everything, I dropped the bucket of popcorn right in front of the counter. I hadn't even taken one step! The lady refilled it with no problem. I spilled it again in the theater when we were taking our seats. Jay offered to take the empty bucket back to the counter and have her refill it again. I told him no because I was embarrassed at this point. He took it anyway and came back with a full bucket of popcorn.

"What did you tell her? I asked.

"*She did it again*," he said.

Sometimes, before or after the movie, I parked at the airport and we watched planes take off and land. We guessed where they came from or where they were going.

I began a long-distance relationship with someone I had worked with in California. I took multiple trips across the country to develop our relationship. We ended up getting married a year and a half later and I moved back to California. I went into marriage wearing blinders and rose-colored glasses; I thought everything was going to work out. I wanted to be married, I wanted to have children, and I wanted to travel—I wanted it all. Unfortunately, I married a man who drank heavily and had other plans. I should say he and his drinking had other plans.

I was thirty-two when we were married in Virginia on a Saturday in February 1982. We flew back to California on Sunday and my husband went to work Monday morning. We had decided to take a honeymoon later on during the spring. I was surprised Monday night when he came home from work, poured ice tea glasses full of vodka and went to bed (or passed out) at eight p.m. It happened every night. I didn't know he drank like this. It was easy to hide in a long distance relationship.

One week later, he was carrying the steaks he had grilled for our dinner when he fell up the steps to our second story apartment. He had been drinking all afternoon and passed out soon after the fall. When he came home from work the next day, I told him I needed to talk to him.

"You've been drunk every day since we've been married," I said. "And I want you to understand that I'm not going to live like this."

"Your mother puts up with it," he said.

"I am not my mother!"

He continued to drink; I sat and watched it day after day. I was still looking through those rose-colored glasses, tolerating it, thinking he would change.

I still grieved and even though I tried to talk to my husband about Richard, it was nonproductive. One time we were at a restaurant and I saw someone who reminded me of Richard. He had black hair with the same cut, wore the same type of glasses, and was about the same height and build.

"He reminds me of Richard," I said casually.

"Was Richard Asian?" my husband asked.

Yes, the man I was looking at was Asian, but still he reminded me of him. Regardless, my husband's insensitive comment hurt.

Another time when we visited my family, my husband said their house looked like a shrine to Richard simply because my mom had a lot of pictures of him on display. I never appreciated his comments about my grief; I felt he rarely had compassion that we had lost my brother. He was just like everyone else who didn't understand or seem to care.

When talking to my husband one day, I told him that I was ready to have a baby. He suggested that we wait until we had been married for a year and then discuss it, to give ourselves some time together before we had an addition to our family. In the meantime, he said I should get a job. That made sense to me so I agreed. I went through an agency and got a job, but one year later, to the day, I brought the subject up again. This time his answer was no, he did not want to have any more children. He had three children from his previous marriage. He was done—another surprise!

The arguments started.

I had a hard time dealing with the fact that I wanted a baby but couldn't have one. The drinking continued as the months passed. The arguments were more frequent and intensified. I became verbally battered and lost in this miserable relationship.

I made an appointment with a Christian counselor and met with him twice.

"Who is going to be the father of your child?" he asked. "You don't have a husband."

The lightbulb came on and the rose-colored glasses came off.

I needed advice and called an 800 number, a support line for families of alcoholics. I didn't need help with an alcoholic. I needed help for someone who drank too much, all the time.

"What do I do to get my husband to stop drinking?" I asked.

After a lengthy conversation, I realized that my husband was an alcoholic and that I couldn't make him stop drinking. "He" had to get help. And, for the first time in my life, I realized that my father's "drinking problem" was alcoholism. I was a little stunned and sad, having to admit it. It sounded so bad.

Our arguments continued, but this time they were about him getting help.

"I don't have a problem, you're the one with the problem," he said.

I realized he wasn't going to get help and I was getting closer to leaving this marriage. I didn't want to because I promised "I will" and "I do" before God and a hundred people. I thought that if he got help, I would stay and try, but he refused.

I left one Sunday afternoon during one his tirades. I would not stay and be battered by this man any longer. I packed one suitcase with clothes, my Bible, and a picture of Jay and Stephanie.

My husband followed me into the garage to my car.

"I don't understand why you're doing this," he said.

"I told you the week after we were married that I wasn't going to live like this and I meant it." I said. "You need to get help."

Thankfully, I had my job. I rented a condo and returned to the church that my husband and I had attended. I made friends with a few women and they frequently invited me to dinner with their families, supporting me through my separation.

I was still grieving. My boss found me crying at my desk one day and was surprised that I wasn't crying because of my separation, but that I was still grieving my little brother.

"Is your husband giving you a difficult time with the divorce?" He asked.

"No." I said.

"What's wrong, why are you crying?"

"My little brother died and I have a hard time with it."

"When did he die?"

"Seven years ago."

"It's been that long and you're still grieving?"

One Saturday, I told one of my friends at church that I had been upset all day, thinking about Richard.

"Maybe he's trying to contact you," she said.

I could tell she had no idea what I was talking about; she could not relate to grief. She was the pastor's wife, and I think because she had been around so much death and attended many funerals she thought she knew all about grief. That is, until the day her mother died.

I didn't see her for two or three weeks after her mother's funeral. She had completely withdrawn and stopped attending church. One day she finally came back to church and approached me after the service. She simply said, "I'm sorry. I didn't know," started crying and walked away. The same thing happened two other times with friends who lost a parent. They came to me and said either, "I want to talk to you because you know what it's like" or "I didn't know."

There is knowledge in grief, knowledge that I don't wish on anyone, but knowledge that everyone will eventually experience at some point in their lives. Without it, people can't relate to those who are grieving. And sometimes, even when they have the knowledge, it's a double-edged sword, because people either want to help or they stay away. The ones who want to help mostly say things that are no help or comfort whatsoever. There are no words that can make anything better or be comforting.

"He's in a better place." I cringed every time I heard it.

"You can't bring him back." Really! What did I say or do to make someone believe that I even thought that was possible?

The people who stay away make the griever feel ignored. The best thing to do, in my opinion, is to just listen to the person grieve, no matter how uncomfortable it is.

The problem with grief so young is that no one your own age knows what you're going through, what you're feeling, or how it's affecting you. Few can associate with it, because few people have experienced it. I was the one who lost my little brother. I was the one who played in the band with him for five years. I was the one who said, "Let's take my car." How many people have ever been in the same situation? My guess is not too many, and certainly no one I knew.

The other problem with grief is that you take it with you wherever you go. It never leaves you alone. The feelings of grief can't be parked somewhere until you have the time and energy to deal with them. They stay inside and keep you twisted. People say that time will heal. Time only teaches you to learn to live without that person in your life.

My mother put a rosebud on Richard's grave every Sunday for years. People told me she needed to stop, she should get counseling. How could they possible know how she felt or what she was going through? I told them she needed to do whatever she needed to do to get through her grief and to leave her alone.

No matter what I did, I carried my grief with me. It had been eight years since Richard's death, and I still had extreme moments of grief. I was never able to contain the emotions that accompanied it. It seemed like a never-ending battle. Would my insides be twisted all of my life?

Then one day, I talked to someone who truly listened. I was grieving and crying, and I finally said it out loud:

"It was my fault."

"It was my fault that Richard wrecked."

"I told him twice to be careful."

"That's the last thing I said to him."

"I don't know why I did, but I did and maybe if I hadn't said it he wouldn't have swerved."

"Maybe he was trying to be careful; maybe he was thinking about my car."

"If I hadn't said it, he would still be alive."

I was immediately assured that it was a natural reaction to swerve and try to miss animals. Anyone would have done the same thing. How many times have we all done it?

"It wasn't your fault."

I finally heard those words. I had held those feelings inside. I had always felt responsible for what happened. I couldn't talk to anyone about it because most people didn't want to hear it, so I could never get to the point of telling anyone what I held inside.

Thankfully, I was able to share it with someone who listened, and once I said it out loud, my insides weren't twisted anymore. I let go of it and had peace with it for the first time since Richard died.

CHAPTER 6

My Children, Too!

———

I WAS BLESSED THE DAY the employment agency sent me to Robertson's Ready Mix, the job my husband insisted I get when I wanted to have a baby. I went there on a temporary assignment to help with a bank reconciliation and was hired as the office manager two months later. I thought managing would be easy and that I knew what I was doing. I knew accounting and I am an organized person; how hard can it be to manage people? But it became evident that I didn't know how to manage people or deal with them properly. I didn't know what I could or couldn't say as a manger in the workplace. I finally admitted I needed help and was ready to improve. I wanted to be good at my job.

George, who worked with us, was my mentor. I always consulted him whenever I had a situation to deal with and was unsure on how to best handle it.

One day I had a meeting with two employees. One of the girls was eating a sandwich while I was trying to discuss something and she clearly wasn't paying any attention to me. I finished the meeting but knew it was not productive. I asked George what I should have said and done. He said I should have ended the meeting as soon as the sandwich appeared and told them we would regroup after she finished eating. How simple was that and I didn't even know?

I went to the self-help section at Barnes and Noble and bought several books whose titles sounded helpful. My boss was going on vacation and asked if I had anything he could read, so I gave him my as yet unread copy of *Bringing Out the Best in People* by Alan Loy McGinnis.

When he returned from vacation, he said, "This is it—this book is what managing people is all about."

He was so impressed with the author that we invited him to come to our company to speak to the entire management team. Alan Loy McGinnis was a pastor whose book was about dealing with people the way Jesus wanted: "Helping other people grow can become life's greatest joy." He autographed my book and wrote, "To Kay, who should get some sort of award for distributing so many of this book." (Yes, he misspelled my name.)

I read a total of thirty-three books when I was learning to deal with people properly. I felt that if I got one thing out of a book that was beneficial to me and helped me as a manager, then it was worth it to have read the entire book. I poured myself into my work, enjoying the challenge, growing as a manager and as a person.

I attended the same church on a regular basis, started getting involved and eventually starting playing the piano for the choir and church services. My friends who supported me after my separation and divorce and I became closer.

Sherry was the pastor's wife. She had a degree in Christian Education, had been a stay-at-home mom for most of her life but had recently graduated from nursing school and was working as a nurse. Claudia was in the education system. She and her husband had both been teachers but she was at a higher level. Claudia asked me to give her piano lessons.

"I feel so blessed to have you as my piano teacher," she said.

"I could bless you more if you practiced," I replied.

Linda and her husband had a car parts business. Vicki had been a stay-at-home mom but had recently returned to work as well.

These ladies along with their families were my closest friends and "church family" in California. I spent most of my time with them, attending church, serving in ministry groups, Bible studies, and other church functions, but I spent my vacation time in Virginia with my family and with Jay and Stephanie.

The year after my divorce I went home in May to celebrate Jay's birthday.

"You came home for Jay's birthday last year so are you going to come home for mine this year?" Stephanie, now six, asked me.

Their birthdays were exactly two weeks apart: Stephanie's was April thirtieth, and Jay's was May fourteenth. I alternated going home for their birthdays and in August I flew them to California to spend a week with me. I went home for a week every year at Christmas.

Christmas was a special time. Our tradition was for the three of us to go shopping together, and then Stephanie and I sat in the middle of my bedroom floor and wrapped presents. She loved Christmas. As a toddler she took her blanket, laid on the floor next to the Christmas tree, and took her nap. When she grew older, she fell asleep on the couch next to the tree. Stephanie could never get close enough to Christmas.

Whenever I went home to visit, Jay and Stephanie joined whoever came to pick me up at the airport. They spent the entire time with me, day and night. I couldn't have loved them more if I'd given birth to them. We became even closer after their parents separated and divorced.

Jay was eight years old the first time he came to California. Sixth months after I was married, he spent two weeks with us, and

I took him to Disneyland, Knott's Berry Farm and the San Diego Zoo. We played in the pool at our condo, went to movies, and played games at Chuck E. Cheese. I loved to play Frogger.

The next time Jay came to California, Stephanie came, too. Everyone was worried; she was a quiet little girl and close to her mother. I was also worried, so I flew to Virginia specifically to fly with them to California. On the plane, Stephanie sat in the window seat, Jay in the middle, and I had the aisle. When the plane took off, Jay and I were anxious to see her reaction.

"Can we go back and do that again?" she said after she watched the runway disappear. Apparently, Stephanie enjoyed flying.

We spent a week together going to all the local amusement parks, seeing movies and swimming in the pool at my condo. When I took them to the airport to return to Virginia, I was sad. I knew when they got home they were going to find out that their parents were going to separate and divorce. I didn't want to let them go; seeing them three times a year was hardly enough.

When Jay was in his teens, he brought friends with him when he and Stephanie visited. One of my favorite stories was about his friend Howard. I was living in a condo at the time, on a golf course with a nearby pond. I took Jay shopping to get a new pair of tennis shoes, and when we returned, I discovered that Howard had popped all of the popcorn I had and he and Stephanie were feeding the ducks, luring them to my condo. After the kids went back to Virginia, the ducks continued to come to my patio looking for popcorn. Duck poop was everywhere! Duck poop was everywhere for days!

The first year Stephanie came without Jay and brought a friend, I asked her what she wanted to do.

"No amusement parks, please!" she said.

"Thank you," I said.

Visiting all the local amusement parks and attractions had been our tradition for many years, but we'd had our fill of them.

It was fun to do different things, girl things. I took them to see plays, including *Beauty and the Beast* and *The Sound of Music*. I took them to have Glamour Shots taken. Stephanie wore a white T-shirt and light blue denim short overalls. After they finished their glamour shots, we walked through the mall.

"Everyone's looking at me," Stephanie said.

"It's because you look like a model," I replied.

After each visit, when I returned home from taking them to the airport, I would find a note either lying on my pillow or on the kitchen counter. It was a thank you for our week of fun from Jay or Stephanie's or one of their friends.

We had a surprise party for Stephanie on her sixteenth birthday. Carmon and Stephanie's friend Martha helped me plan it. Jay took his sister to a movie that afternoon. We started decorating when they left. Her friends arrived, parked their cars behind Carmon's house and gathered in the basement waiting to surprise her. When they got home from the movie, Jay followed Stephanie down the basement steps.

"Surprise!" everyone yelled.

The look on her face told me she wasn't too surprised. I found out later that Jay's girlfriend had asked Stephanie if she was happy that her aunt was going to come home for her birthday. She may not have been surprised, but Stephanie walked over to me and said, "I feel loved." What a sweet moment.

In May of the next year, my father was hospitalized and died on May 13, the day before Jay's birthday. My dad was seventy-five. He had been in and out of the hospital several times in the past few years, dealing with leukemia and congestive heart failure.

Carmon went early on that Sunday morning to be with our dad in the Veterans Hospital in Salem, Virginia. Jay relieved him sometime before lunch. My mom and I arrived in the early afternoon to relieve Jay and spend the rest of the day with my dad. We left that night and were on our way down the hall when I asked my mom to wait while I went back into his room. We had only just said goodbye but I wanted to assure him that we would be back early the next morning. He had turned in the bed and was laying with his back to me.

"We'll be back, and I'll see you in the morning," I said.

"Okay, sweet pea." That's what he called me.

God has a way of granting small gifts, and this was one He gave to me. There had been tense moments growing up in an alcoholic environment but there were also sweet memories, one of which was my dad calling me "Sweet pea." I thought it was his way of telling me he loved me.

My regret is that I didn't stay with him that night. The hospital called a few hours later, around one in the morning, to let us know that my dad died. Carmon came over as soon as my mom called, and the three of us hugged. It was a surreal moment; Richard should have been there with us.

A little while later that same night, my dad's cousin Allen called to let us know that he visited my dad soon after we left. He went there purposely to ask him if he'd ever given his life to Christ. My dad told him yes, one night when he was sitting in his chair in the den watching Billy Graham on TV. At the end of the service when the invitation was given, he made the decision.

'Why didn't I know that?

I was comforted knowing Richard wasn't alone anymore. I don't know why I thought he was in heaven by himself, but now my dad was with him, and it made me feel better that they were together. I took it for granted that when my dad died he went to heaven. Why hadn't I been the one to ask him if he had given his life to Christ? I felt bad that I hadn't, that I didn't know, had only assumed, but was comforted with Allen's news.

Because music had been such a large part of our lives and something that I shared with my dad, I played the piano at his funeral. I played a medley of "The Old Rugged Cross" and "Amazing Grace," the two hymns he always wanted to play with Richard and me.

For the first time, Jay, twenty-two, and Stephanie, seventeen, experienced the grief of losing a close family member. I think it was hardest on Jay; he and my dad had been buddies. Jay and Stephanie never saw his personality change when he drank. My dad had always been their loving and doting "Pa."

Stephanie graduated high school and attended Roanoke College. Jay was attending Ferrum College and his visits to California weren't as consistent. He came a few times during his college years, once bringing three friends. I took them to Las Vegas and we played craps. Jay rolled the dice for about a half hour one day and everyone cheered each time he rolled as it was usually a winning number. People were tipping him because they were making money on Jay's good luck.

During the summer between Stephanie's junior and senior years of college, she was trying to find an internship. I told her if she wanted to, she and a friend could come to California and work with me. I was actually being selfish because if she took the offer, she would live with me during her internship. A few weeks later Stephanie and her step-sister Dee flew to California to live and work with me for two months. I was surprised when I learned that Dee was coming with her. I knew they had been friends for a long time and were now step-sisters, but I didn't know how close they were. I asked Stephanie how she and Dee became such good friends, and she said Dee, whose parents were also divorced, was the only person who spoke to her at the new school she had to attend in the second grade after Carmon and her mother separated. Carmon and Jennifer, Dee's mom, began dating and were married during the girls' freshman year of college. Stephanie and Dee claimed responsibility for getting them together.

We worked during the week and on the weekends had fun. Stephanie used one of my calendars and marked it with our plans. We made day visits to Pasadena, Universal Studios, Newport Beach, and Costa Mesa, attended a Dixie Chicks concert and several plays, celebrated July 4th, and had a scrapbook party. Stephanie and Dee went to church with me every Sunday during those two months. On the week nights when we stayed at home, putting jigsaw puzzles together and eating Wilderness Raspberry Sherbet. They both enjoyed cooking our dinners, even though sometimes that meant cereal.

The major fun started on July 14th when I took Stephanie and Dee to Las Vegas. Stephanie was twenty-one but Dee was only twenty. It's only about a three-hour drive from my house. I drove so the girls could see the desert.

The first thing we did after checking into Mandalay Bay was walk through some of the casinos.

"I've never been anywhere like this before," Stephanie said.

The first casino we went in was New York, New York. I gave Stephanie twenty dollars to use on a giant slot machine. Over the next two or three minutes she won about eighty dollars. But as almost everyone who goes gambling knows, easy come, easy go. Over the next two or three minutes, her winnings were gone.

The next night Stephanie, Dee and I went to the Cirque du Soleil show *O,* a water-themed stage production at the Bellagio

Hotel. We sat in the second row and were given towels in case of splashing water. After the show we decided to play craps at Mandalay Bay. Stephanie stood next to the table boss and he taught her how to bet. Dee stood on the opposite side of the table looking guilty because she wasn't twenty-one. We played craps until about two in the morning.

Stephanie's entry on the calendar for July 17th was "Jaybird Arrives."

We had called Jay "Jaybird" ever since he was a toddler. The nickname seemed to fit him more when he was younger, but we still used it.

I was in Virginia when Jay was probably twelve, and Stephanie and I went to one of his basketball games. He was dribbling the ball and racing down the court when I stood up and yelled, "Go Jaybird!"

"Don't…say…Jaybird," Stephanie said.

She was seven, and I guess I embarrassed her or maybe she was protecting her brother from being embarrassed. There were hardly any people at this game and even in my soft voice, as hard as I was trying to yell, she was afraid the few people who were there may have heard me.

Jay (AKA Jaybird), along with his girlfriend, arrived on July 17th. They drove across country because Jay would be attending the Thomas Jefferson School of Law in San Diego that fall. His girlfriend stayed for another day and then flew back to Virginia.

That Friday morning, July 22, Jay left for San Diego with Stephanie, Dee, and my credit card. He called a couple of hours later to tell me he had checked into a resort near the beach.

I met them for dinner and then Jay, Stephanie, and Dee went to a party that one of his friends was having. When they came back to the hotel, Dee and I went to bed, but Jay and Stephanie went out to the area next to our room, a walkway of sorts. Jay sat in a chair and Stephanie sat at his feet; they talked, laughed, and were clearly having quality time together. As I lay awake in bed, I enjoyed watching them.

Jay stayed in San Diego with a friend, and on Sunday afternoon the girls and I went back to Riverside to await my mom.

My mother's family (The Crooks) had a reunion almost every year, and this year it was in Pincher Creek, Canada. My mother was in her late seventies, and most of the family members were her cousins. She flew to California by herself, and we picked her up at the Ontario airport. Two days later, we flew to Calgary, Canada. When we landed, Stephanie was behind me as we walked down the concourse.

"I hate this country," Stephanie said.

"How can you hate this county when you just got here?" I asked.

I already knew the answer. She was ready to go home to Virginia. Visiting Canada wasn't part of Stephanie and Dee's original plan. I asked them to stay the extra days and go with us. They were ready to go home, see their friends and boyfriends and get ready for their senior year in college.

The day after we flew back to California, Jay came from San Diego. We had one more day together before my mom, Stephanie, and Dee had to leave, and we spent it at home relaxing. The next morning they flew out of John Wayne airport in Orange County. When we left for the airport, Jay also left for San Diego. My summer with Stephanie was over, and my time with Jay living in California was just beginning.

It was exciting to have Jay live so close, knowing that I could see him more frequently than three times a year for a week at a time. We enjoyed movies, dinners and basically just spending time together on weekends.

The next year, during spring break of her senior year in college, Stephanie and several of her friends came to California and stayed with Jay in San Diego. We made plans for them to meet me at the Pantages Theater and see *The Lion King*.

Jay drove from San Diego, and I waited for them in front of the theatre. He came around the corner of Argyle Ave. and Hollywood Boulevard, pulled to the curb, and he and Stephanie jumped out of his car. We quickly ran into the theatre only minutes before the play started. Our seats were in the section to the right of the stage in row RR. Jay sat in the aisle seat, Stephanie next to him, and I sat next to Stephanie. During the opening number, the animals started coming down the aisles. I nudged Stephanie and pointed them out to her.

"We're going to come to some more of these," Jay said, when the song ended.

"No," Stephanie said.

She didn't want us to go to plays without her. What she didn't know was that if we went to any other plays, I intended to fly her to California so the three of us could see them together.

From the moment Jay and Stephanie were born, I felt as though they were my children, too. They called me Katie when they were little but it changed to Kaye during their pre-teen years. Stephanie started calling me Clark, my given middle name, when she was in college. The only time I was their "aunt" ("Kaye my aunt" instead of "Aunt Kaye") was when they introduced me to someone.

Jay was outgoing and affectionate. He always gave hello hugs and said goodbye with another hug and a kiss on the check. He loved people and never met a stranger; it seemed that everyone he met became his friend. Regardless of how old he was or where we were, Jay always ran into one of his "buddies." We were in the lobby of the Mandalay Bay in Las Vegas when, to our surprise, we heard someone shout, "Hey, Bennett." I thought to myself, *You've got to be kidding*. It was another one of his buddies.

Stephanie was quiet and not affectionate, but her beautiful smile and sweet spirit radiated whenever she entered a room. I used to tease her and tell her that her first words were, "No hugs, no kisses." She actually said that when she was a toddler. When she was a teenager, I explained to her that a hug was not a pat on the back; it was body contact and a squeeze. She became more outgoing in high school and was voted "Best Personality" by her senior class.

Driving home that night after the play and dinner, I wondered when the three of us would be able to spend time together again. Jay would graduate from law school in a year or so and Stephanie would graduate from college in only two or three months. Once they began their careers, their vacation time would be limited. I imagined their next visits would probably include Jay's girlfriend, Stephanie's boyfriend, and eventually their spouses.

As it turned out, the day we met at the Pantages Theater and saw *The Lion King* was the last time the three of us would share special time together in California.

CHAPTER 7

The Day of Infamy

———

AFTER THEIR COLLEGE GRADUATIONS IN 2001, Stephanie and Dee moved to Raleigh, North Carolina and started looking for jobs. I went home the week of Labor Day for my mom's birthday. Our birthdays are two days apart, hers the fifth and mine the seventh of September. We drove to Raleigh to spend a day with Stephanie.

"Doesn't it look good?" Stephanie asked as she showed us her apartment. It was in a beautiful wooded area, and behind the complex was a lake with a track for walking or running. She told me there had been two assaults and a rape at the track—that wasn't good news. Their apartment was on the first floor of a three-story building. They were supposed to be on the second floor, but the apartment wasn't ready and after a week in a hotel, they were offered one on the first floor. We took Stephanie shopping and bought some things for her bedroom and then we took both girls to lunch. Later that afternoon, my mom and I drove back to Rocky Mount.

Stephanie didn't have a job at the time we visited her, but a few days later, on my birthday, she called to say she had a job with IBM.

"They want me, Kaye! I have a job. They want me," she said.

I was so happy for her and hearing the excitement in her voice was one of my best birthday presents. Shortly after she began the job, I started getting e-mails from her every morning. She told me about her day, her job, the apartment, and, of course, her boyfriend.

I looked forward to hearing the familiar ding, knowing that I just received an e-mail message from her. One day she said she received an award for an accomplishment at work and got a paid day off.

"You are so like me," I said in my reply along with my congratulations. The same thing happened at my first job; I received the acknowledgement but did not get the paid day off.

One day in her e-mail she told me that a neighbor called the police because she saw someone looking into Stephanie's bedroom window. I immediately called her to get more information. The police advised Stephanie to keep her window closed and the blinds drawn. She liked to keep the window open a little for the fresh air. They were also trying to save money on the electric bill. I told her that she had to get out of the apartment, and she agreed. Thankfully, the girls had plans to move a few weeks later when the lease ended. Dee made plans to move to Richmond, Virginia. Their roommate Emily planned on moving back to Virginia, and Stephanie intended to move to Charleston, South Carolina.

During the week prior to May 21, Dee's father died, so she was in Rocky Mount. Emily had gone to Virginia for the week. Stephanie had been in Charleston over the weekend to visit her boyfriend but was back at work on Monday. I called her from work Monday evening to see how she was doing, and she said she was tired. I asked her if she was tired from the weekend trip or if it was just "Monday tired." We talked for a few minutes and I questioned whether she was okay to stay in the apartment by herself. She said yes. However, I had the feeling she was a little scared to be there alone. I was interrupted and had to end the call.

At work the next morning I didn't hear the familiar ding. I thought Stephanie must have been busy and hadn't had time to e-mail, so I didn't e-mail her either. After lunch, there was still no e-mail but I had a call from my mother. She was scared and upset. Carmon had called to let her know that Stephanie hadn't come to work and the police couldn't find her. I asked my mom a couple of questions but she didn't know anything. She said Carmon was on his way to Raleigh. She asked me not to call Carmon because their conversation hadn't gone well. Carmon was in shock and upset. My mom didn't want me to bother him.

Stephanie was missing, the police were involved, and don't call Carmon! It was only moments from the time I hung up the phone with my mother that I had a call from him.

"It's Stephanie," he said.

"Carmon, is she all right?" I asked.

"She's dead," he said.

"What!"

"She's dead. I'm going to call Jay next. I want you and Jay to fly home together."

"We will."

I bent over, my arm on the corner of my desk. I probably looked like I was vomiting into the trashcan. The second I heard she was dead I went into shock. I didn't have time to wrap my mind around what I'd just heard and didn't even ask Carmon what happened. He hadn't volunteered any information—the call was over. Thoughts of the Peeping Tom were lingering in the back of my mind.

Stephanie was gone. How was that possible? I thought about Jay and how hard this would be for him. I lost my little brother and now he was going to have to go through the loss of his little sister. I couldn't imagine Carmon having to make the call to his son. I thought about my dad and was grateful he had already passed so he wouldn't have to deal with this. I thought about my mom, afraid she wouldn't survive it. I thought about how the next year was going to be without Stephanie. The first year after losing someone was the worst.

The next call I received was from Jay. He was crying, and I assured him that we would get home. I would take care of it and let him know the plans. He had asked Carmon what happened, but Carmon told him he would tell us more when we got home.

I finally walked out of my office to get help. Thankfully, Dave, my coworker, was in the hall walking toward me.

"Stephanie's dead, Stephanie's dead," I said desperately.

He took me back to my office, and I called Dennis, my boss, to let him know. I didn't have the answers to his questions about what happened. He had someone call to get flights for Jay and me to go home. I called Claudia and Sherry; Claudia met me at my home and helped me pack.

Dennis and Dave drove me to San Diego. I sat in the back seat, in shock and crying. We were about halfway there when Jay called and told me someone broke into Stephanie's apartment that night and killed her.

"How do you know that?" I heard my voice get louder when I asked him.

"I talked to Dee, and she told me," he said.

I couldn't think; I could hardly speak. I told Jay we would be there soon.

"Someone broke into her apartment and killed her. Why would somebody do that?" I told Dennis and Dave as I heard my voice get even louder.

During the next few minutes my world was reduced to the size of the space I occupied in the back seat of the car. I was launched into an unbelievable state of shock. Never in my life have I cried so hard; I gasped for breath. It was beyond shock, beyond pain, beyond agony; it was nearly unbearable. I sat and hung my head; I didn't know what to do with my hands. There were no words to describe the feeling of hearing the news that someone murdered Stephanie. I was physically ill.

Jay walked out on the lawn as we pulled into the street in front of his apartment. We hugged, then said goodbye to Dennis and Dave. Several of Jay's friends stayed with us until we left for the airport. Jay's girlfriend flew with us on our redeye flight out of San Diego to Dulles airport in Washington, DC. None of us had slept. While we waited for our connecting flight, Jay's girlfriend went to get water for us. Jay, lying on the floor next to my chair, looked up at me and said, "I wish I was Superman and able to turn back time, to be there and help Stephanie."

"I wish you could, too," I said.

Carmon's brother-in-law, Kevin, picked us up in Roanoke and we drove to Carmon's home. Several of Stephanie's friends and some of our family members were there.

"Our girl, our girl…" I said when I hugged Carmon.

Dee sat in a large leather chair, crying. She looked at me and asked, "Why Stephanie?" I didn't have an answer.

A few minutes later, I asked her how Stephanie died. Dee couldn't bring herself to say the words, but she held her hand up to her throat.

Stephanie had been strangled.

Jay stayed at Carmon's for a while then he left to go to his mother's house. I went to pick up my mom and bring her to Carmon's. He hadn't told her that Stephanie died because she was by herself. He called our aunt, my mother's sister, and asked her to stay with my mom.

Our family viewed Stephanie's body two days later on the morning of the visitation. It was a relief to see that the only visible injury was a deep cut in her chin, but at the same time it was unnerving. Jay asked to view his sister by himself. I can only imagine the things he said to her and the pain I knew he must be feeling because he'd lost his little sister. I knew the pain of losing a younger sibling but couldn't imagine how he felt, coupling that loss with the added nightmare of her murder. Stephanie's boyfriend was with us and he also asked to view Stephanie by himself.

Carmon decided to have the casket closed during the visitation and open it afterward for Stephanie's friends to say goodbye; that turned out to be a wise decision. The funeral director told us someone came by earlier during the day to "see the girl that was murdered."

The visitation was held in the chapel of the funeral home. We were to receive people starting at five. We arrived at four-thirty and a line had already formed. Stephanie's maternal grandparents were the first in the receiving line. Jay stood between his mother and Carmon in front of the casket and Jennifer, Carmon's wife, stood next to him. I stood next to Jennifer, and Stephanie's boyfriend stood between me and my mother.

I was impressed by Stephanie's friends. It seemed as though someone gave them specific instructions on how to act, how to dress, and what to say. They each introduced themselves, explained how they knew Stephanie, and expressed their sympathy. A lot of adults don't know how to dress appropriately or act, but these young adults were amazing. After they spoke to my mother, all of Jay and Stephanie's friends sat in the pews in front of us, waiting to say goodbye to Stephanie.

My friend's behavior, on the other hand, was not as respectful.

After I learned of Stephanie's death and had flown to Virginia, Linda called to tell me three of them were coming to attend the funeral. She and Claudia had frequent flyer miles on different airlines and were trying to find flights. Vicki was trying in some way to get a flight, and Sherry would not be able to come because she couldn't afford it and didn't have any frequent flyer miles. I offered the use of my frequent flyer miles if anyone needed them, and I gave her my frequent flyer number and password. I particularly meant the miles for Sherry.

My four friends arrived in time for the visitation at the funeral home. However, they did not act like they had traveled across country to support a friend who had lost a niece to murder. They acted like they were fourteen-years-old and were away from home for the first time on a field trip.

Three of them came in the chapel that night, cut through the line of visitors, walked up the center isle and sat on the front row pew in front of me; although Vicki never came inside. She sat outside on a bench talking on her cell phone to her daughter who was at a Kenny Chesney concert. My friends took every opportunity to introduce themselves as "Kaye's friends from California." They laughed and were as giddy as schoolgirls. They eventually left while we were still in the receiving line.

Once the line of visitors was depleted, our receiving line disbursed. I walked to the back of the chapel and sat by myself. Stephanie's casket was opened; I watched as her friends slowly walked toward it together. Seeing them stand next to their friend and listening to them cry when they saw her was one of the saddest things I've seen. Because of their young age, it was probably their first experience with death. I knew all too well what it was like, and my heart went out to them.

They were still standing next to the casket when I walked up to say goodbye to Stephanie. I noticed there was a ring on her finger. Stephanie's boyfriend had bought it for her. It wasn't a diamond but a band that had particular meaning for them. Stephanie had told me about the ring, and I believe it had been her birthday present; he was getting it sized at the time. When we viewed her body in the morning, her hands were folded and bare, but now the band was on her finger. Her boyfriend had also told me, while we were in the receiving line, that he had planned on asking Stephanie to marry him soon.

Stephanie's casket was closed and we left.

Typically, funerals are held on the third day after the death, but Stephanie's funeral was delayed for an additional day because her body had been at Duke University Medical Center for the autopsy. Carmon chose to have only a graveside service. When we left the funeral home on the way to the cemetery, the police controlled the traffic. Just like at Richard's funeral, they saluted as we passed. How respectful that they saluted a young, innocent girl who had been murdered, whose life had been taken.

The Roanoke College chaplain led the service. I couldn't imagine what a pastor would say at the service of someone who had been murdered.

"There are three things in life that are certain: good, evil, and beauty." "Good is God and His promise of salvation, evil is the darkness that took the life a young girl, and beauty was Stephanie," the chaplain said.

When I heard those words, I felt a momentary sense of peace and calm. This man got it. I've been to funerals where the pastor just goes through the motions of a funeral without any real connection to the deceased or their family and the service was impersonal and awkward. Stephanie's death must have had an impact on the chaplain because he opened the service with such a simple but powerful statement.

Stephanie was murdered on May 21, 2002. She was buried four days later on May 25, next to Richard on the anniversary of his death, in a grave that was originally intended for my use when the time came. She was twenty-three years old.

Our family sat in chairs in front of the casket during the service. When the service ended we stood up and walked away. I found myself standing next to the chaplain.

"How do you forgive someone who does this type of thing?" I asked him.

The chaplain didn't answer.

Jay was standing next to me.

"I'm so proud of you," I said. "The eulogy you wrote and gave during the service was really nice, and you did a good job."

I gave him a hug and then I felt a hand on my arm. Sherry pulled me from Jay and away from the chaplain over to where people were standing. "Dennis came here from California," she said. The two of us probably looked like school children, one pulling the other one across a playground. I was embarrassed. Why did she need to attract so much attention?

We left the cemetery and went to a local church that wanted to provide a meal for our family. Almost everyone from the service came and after the meal we went to Carmon's home. Dennis and his family asked if I would show them were I was raised before they left for the airport. I took them to see my mom's home and then gave them a quick, ten minute tour around the town of Rocky Mount. We went back to Carmon's home and they left to return to California.

My friends also wanted a tour and had asked me to meet them at their hotel. I picked them up and then went to my mom's house.

Then I gave them the tour of Rocky Mount, but they wanted more. I spent the next two hours touring my friends around the surrounding area. I drove on some of the backroads so they could see the county.

"What do you think about the scenery? Sherry asked.

"It's hard to see anything because Kaye's driving so fast," Linda said.

I slowed down and tried to give them a tour before I took them back to their hotel. It was a relief when I was able to go home. It took too much energy being their tour guide. They may have felt like they were on vacation but I certainly didn't. I would love to have given them a tour some other time when my heart was in it, but today wasn't that day.

Stephanie and Jay's friends had been at Carmon's that afternoon and I wasn't able to be with them. Being around them made me feel close to Stephanie, and I wouldn't have the opportunity again any time soon.

CHAPTER 8
The Aftermath of Murder

———

THE INVESTIGATION INTO STEPHANIE'S MURDER began. The Raleigh Police wanted to interview Stephanie's family members. On Tuesday of the week after the funeral, the detective in charge of major crimes and another officer, the police psychologist, came to Carmon's home. They spoke to us first as a group, and then we were interviewed individually.

When they spoke to us as a group, the psychologist explained how they knew we would have questions about the murder, but it would be best for us if they didn't tell us everything at that time. The information would be too much for us to bear because we already had enough to deal with. I felt relieved in a way because he was right; I couldn't have dealt with it. But a lingering gloom existed that assured us we were going to be subjected to more bad news.

He also said to not blame ourselves because each one of us would feel we could have prevented this from happening if we'd only said or done something different. He assured us the only person responsible for Stephanie's death was the person who broke into her apartment and killed her.

As he spoke, I silently nodded in agreement. I was the last person in our family to talk to Stephanie. I asked her if she was okay to stay in the apartment by herself. She had said yes.

I should have said, "Get out of the apartment. Go to a hotel, and I'll pay for it. Don't stay there by yourself." But I didn't say any of those things.

The psychologist suggested we read the Book of Job. I was startled by his suggestion. Read Job? I've read Job and, yes, Job lost everything, but he had a happy ending; God gave him double what he'd lost. We'd never get Stephanie back. No thank you to that advice.

He also warned us about anger and to not take our anger out on the people we loved. I didn't understand what he meant. When Richard died, we weren't angry with each other. Why would we be angry now?

My individual interview with the chief detective went like this:

"Kaye, would you consider yourself Stephanie's surrogate mother?" the detective asked.

"In some ways, yes," I said.

"So would you say that you and Stephanie were close?"

"Yes."

"Can you tell us what you and Stephanie had in common?"

"We both liked to read."

"What did you read?"

"*Harry Potter*, *To Kill a Mockingbird*…" I started naming books.

"Novels?"

"Yes, novels."

"Can you tell us where Stephanie and her friends hung out?"

"Not really."

"Why not?"

"Well, I wasn't here. I don't really know. I'm sorry. It's just that we lost our little brother from a car accident when he was nineteen. A dog ran out in front of him, and he was killed instantly. This is so different."

"Yes, it is, Kaye. This is murder," the police psychologist said.

The detective continued to ask questions, but I had no helpful information. He quickly realized it and my interview was over. Usually in these situations, the interviews with immediate family members reveal information about the people in the victim's life that would lead them to a suspect. What they didn't understand, but would learn over time, was that Stephanie did not live a life-style that attracted danger.

If the detectives had been at the visitation, they would have met Stephanie's friends. They would have seen how well they were dressed, and how well they handled themselves. These were the people in Stephanie's life. These were the people Stephanie "hung out with."

I didn't want to know any of the bad things and was afraid to find them out. Jay, on the other hand, wanted to know everything. His interview was after mine. He came out of it, looked straight at me, and said, "She was raped." He had asked them. I was already in a state of shock, but this news sent me to a new level, as I'm sure it did all of us. The expression on Jay's face said it all—shock, pain, anger.

After our interviews, the detectives left. My sister-in-law told me that she and the detective accompanied Stephanie's boyfriend to the doctor's office where she worked to obtain a pubic hair sample for DNA testing; they had to rule him out as part of the investigation. They weren't specifically told at the time about the rape, but she and Carmon had assumed as much. I'm sure they didn't say anything because they were trying to protect us.

Carmon did tell me that the murderer used the window to break into her apartment. Because it wasn't installed properly and even though it appeared locked from the inside, it could still be opened from the outside. There was nothing obstructing a possible intruder, and the shrubbery at the apartment complex was overgrown. It provided protection for someone who didn't want to be seen.

Those girls hadn't been safe from the moment they moved in.

When I went back to my mother's house, she was in an ill mood; everything she said was filled with anger. Was she upset because she had been left alone all day and had not been involved in the interviews? Was this her grief unleashing itself and she was using me as her sounding board? Was this the anger the police psychologist had warned us about? I couldn't deal with it and definitely could not bring myself to share the news that her granddaughter had been raped.

After hearing the news about the rape, I felt as though the life had been beaten out of me. Now having to deal with my mother's rage, I felt as if I was going to break. I was about to crumble. I went outside and sat on the front stoop and called a friend to hear a calm and reassuring voice. When he answered the phone, I was choking back my emotions as I told him about the day's events. And then, I said it. Something I wouldn't say out loud again for over a year.

"She was raped."

I wanted to hear, "I'm so sorry" or "Oh, no." Instead I heard, "Of course she was. That's why he killed her, so she wouldn't be able to identify him."

How is it possible that people can discuss the rape of my niece so casually?

When there's a death in the family, it's the custom to receive food from friends and family. Carmon's home was flooded with food, and at my mother's we had received more than the two of us could possibly consume. One friend, who had nothing but good intentions, brought a complete meal to my mother's home. This particular friend assured us that Stephanie had been raped. Our response was that we didn't know; no one had told us anything. She again assured us she was raped because she knew someone who knew someone at the Raleigh police department who confirmed it.

"Oh yes, she was definitely raped!" she insisted.

How could this person casually but firmly assure us that our beautiful, sweet-spirited Stephanie had been raped? How could she be saying these things to us? How could she be using her name and the word *rape* in the same sentence? Only two days earlier we learned that she was dead, had been murdered, and now these things are being said to us. My mind would not let me go there. *I am not going to believe it. It's not true. They don't know.*

I had been holding onto the hope that they were all wrong, that it was just gossip and speculation. Unfortunately, they did know. As we found out that day during the interviews with the Raleigh detectives, it was true.

That would not be the end of the bad news.

After two weeks, I returned to California and went back to work. Although I attended work, my mind, body, and spirit were depleted. Each day when I woke up, I wondered how I would get up and make it through another day. It seemed miraculous to me when I watched one foot touch the floor, the other foot follow, and how I slowly started walking and then went through the motions of getting ready for work. Somehow I ended up at work to sit through another day. At night when I went to bed, I was amazed that I made it through the day and wondered how I would be able to do it again tomorrow.

Every day I waited for the phone call from Carmon to hear him say, "They've caught the guy, and he's been arrested." I wanted to know everything the Raleigh police were doing, but I didn't want to bother him with daily phone calls, so I constantly checked the Internet for any current news reports. On the days and weeks immediately following the murder, the articles appeared frequently.

As the days passed, my ability to get through the day and actually start doing my job began to improve. I felt I had reached the point where I could smile my way through things and give the impression that I was okay and no one could tell what I was going through. The people I worked with came in my office periodically throughout each day to spend time with me and make sure I was all right.

"Don't look at the Internet," Dennis said one day when he came in my office. I noticed he looked anxious.

"Okay." I said. But I knew I would check for any news updates.

That same day the visits from my coworkers were more frequent, although I didn't notice it at the time. Oblivious to what was going on, I clicked on the Internet for the Raleigh news. I only saw three words that sent me into yet another state of shock: bound and gagged. I quickly closed the browser and ran to the bathroom so no one could see me as I tried to breathe and began to cry.

After a while I gathered myself and went back to my desk. I sat there in a daze for the remainder of the day.

"I told you to not look at the Internet," Dennis said.

How could I not look? My niece had been murdered, and I wanted to know about the investigation. I wanted the guy—the monster—caught.

It was obvious to everyone that I was upset, but I made it through the remainder of the day in what seemed like a blur. That night at home, I broke down. My heart was torn and every fiber of my being was in a state of unbelievable shock and despair. What else had happened to her? What else did she have to endure? These questions were in my mind, but I could not let myself think of the possibilities. It was literally too much to bear.

The next day was Saturday, and I went through all of my pictures and gathered every one of Stephanie I could find. I cradled them in my arms as I rocked back and forth on the couch, sobbing, trying in some way to help her, trying to make the impossible happen, and will myself to be there that night to help her.

I started having nightmares. One dream was of Stephanie lying in her coffin and trying to talk to us. In another dream, she was standing near me, pointing out the places on her hip and back where the murderer had hurt her.

Through all of this, my mind and body only let me deal with one thing at a time. I don't know if it was because I was in different states of shock during the time frame from her death to the day I learned that Stephanie had been bound and gagged, but I was thankful that shock, in its own way, seemed to build walls around my immediate state of mind. It's almost as if everything else I had been dealing with up to that point was suddenly parked somewhere until I could get through the most recent knowledge and then cope with everything again.

CHAPTER 9
Intense Anger

———

IMAGINE A LAKE WITH WATER so calm it has the appearance of glass. Imagine the peaceful feeling you have sitting next to it. Maybe in the distance someone is fishing in a small boat with a single line cast into the water. Perhaps it's at night, the moonlight is reflecting on the water, and the only sound you hear is the chorus of the crickets or the soft lapping of water against the shore.

Now imagine the same lake and someone drops a Volkswagen Beetle in the middle of it, causing storm-like waves. The fishing boat capsizes. Even after the waves subside, large rings of water continuously ripple. It takes a long time for the lake to become calm again. Someone throws a rock into the middle of the lake and small rings of water appear.

The lake was my life—calm, serene, happy. Jay was attending law school in San Diego, and I enjoyed having him only a couple hours away. I saw him every other week or so when I'd drive to San Diego and take him to dinner or he would come to Riverside and spend the weekend with me. We had been to several concerts, many movies, and even made a weekend trip to Las Vegas. Stephanie graduated from Roanoke College and started her career in Raleigh. We shared e-mails every day about her new job and apartment. She and her boyfriend were getting serious. I was hopeful that they would soon be engaged and that I could help her plan her wedding.

We were making plans for a shopping weekend in Raleigh.

Stephanie and I were also making plans for her and her boyfriend to visit in August. She wanted him to experience California and take him to see *The Lion King*. She would say, "He just doesn't know," meaning he'd never been to a play of that caliber. I enjoyed her excitement.

The news that Stephanie died was the Volkswagen dropped into my life. The storm-like waves followed. She was murdered. She was raped. She was bound and gagged. The continuous never-ending rings of water were the constant things that accompany a murder investigation and the effects of evil on the lives of the people—Stephanie's family and friends—who loved and cared about her. These were the things that caused the anger to build and grow. This was the anger the police psychologist warned us about that day.

When I came home from work every day, grateful to have the day behind me, I sat at the horseshoe-shaped bar in my home, scrapbook supplies and the pictures I'd taken on my recent trip to England spread out around me. I went through the motions of scrapbooking. Sometimes I just sat and stared at the page. Some nights I accomplished something, sometimes not. Sometimes I ate dinner, sometimes not.

But every night without exception, I drank beer. Sometimes I'd drink just one, sometimes four, but never more than four. Stephanie's boyfriend fulfilled the plans they had made and came to California that summer. Jay, his girlfriend, and Stephanie's boyfriend saw the large, green trashcan in my garage full of beer bottles and asked if I'd had a party. I drank beer for four to five months after I came back to California. Why beer? I don't know; I never drank much of it before. It took the edge off of every twisted nerve in my body and helped me cope for a few hours until bedtime. I cried every night.

And every night the phone rang; I knew before I answered it that it was one of my friends. Maintaining a friendship takes energy. Grief takes energy. Grief and murder were taking all of my energy. I didn't have enough left over on a daily basis after work to do anything but try to maintain until bedtime. It seemed like each night one of my friends called to talk, much more so than they ever had before. And when I say talk, I mean I mainly listened to the never-ending chatter on the other end of the phone. I'm basically a quiet person, and talking on the phone has never been something I've done or liked to do.

I know these friends meant well and were concerned about me. But when someone is grieving, people should listen to what the grieving person is saying. The Bible is specific about this point:

"When three of Job's friends heard of all the tragedy that had befallen him, they got in touch with each other and traveled from their homes to comfort and console him. Their names were Eliphaz the Temanite, Bildad the Shuhite, and Zophar the Naamathite. Job was so changed that they could scarcely recognize him. Wailing loudly in despair, they tore their robes and threw dust into the air and put earth on their heads to demonstrate their sorrow. Then they sat upon the ground with him silently for seven days and nights, no one speaking a word; for they saw that his suffering was too great for words." *Job 2: 11–13*

This is grief; suffering too great for words. How do you support someone who is grieving? *Sit with them silently, not speaking a word, for their suffering is too great for words.* This is the opposite of constant chatter. Two of my friends were the ones making the majority of the phone calls. One by one I told them that I needed time; that I just needed to be left alone. They didn't listen to me; they didn't hear anything I said. I listened to their constant chatter, but they paid no attention to me, to my heart, to my needs.

Ever since Stephanie was a little girl I took her shopping for clothes. We would scour the store and select a lot of things to take into the dressing room. Some of the things I selected for her were for fun, just to try them on and see what they were like. As she tried each one on, we would decide "not a good one" or "this could be the one." After she tried everything on, we got rid of the no's and retried the possible ones, eventually selecting something to purchase. After she grew up, I enjoyed hearing her tell stories about the times I took her shopping when she was little.

We had planned a shopping weekend in Raleigh. I knew that with her first job and apartment she wouldn't have a lot of extra money for clothes, so when she suggested I come to Raleigh and see the new shopping center and go to Nordstrom, I knew I would have the opportunity to treat her to another shopping experience. My plan was to buy whatever she wanted—if it was a new wardrobe, that's what I would buy. Stephanie was not the kind of person to take advantage of anyone's generosity; she was always thoughtful and conservative about the money being spent. She made wise decisions as a shopper.

During one of my friend's phone calls, the conversation turned to shopping and she asked if I was going to the semi-annual sale at Nordstrom. I couldn't believe what I was hearing. It was the same weekend I was supposed to go to Raleigh and shop with Stephanie, and this friend knew it. My friend was trying so hard to keep the conversation going, and I'm assuming it was to keep my mind off my grieving and loss, if only for a little while. What she didn't realize was that she was doing more harm than good, and I didn't have the patience to deal with much more.

The last time she called, the talking continued, but when I didn't respond to anything she said, she asked what was wrong.

"You don't listen to me. You don't stop talking," I said.

"I do not," she said defiantly.

That was the last time we talked. I guess the word spread because I didn't get any more telephone calls from anyone. I finally had the alone time I had been asking for.

I felt bad that I might have hurt their feelings, but they didn't exactly follow the lesson in Job about grief: "Then they sat upon the ground with him silently for seven days and nights, no one speaking a word; for they saw that his suffering was too great for words" *Job 2:13*. I'm not sure if they could tell my suffering was too great for words since they were never around me. They asked to visit, but I always said no. I didn't have the energy for it. They didn't see how my nose bled during extremely difficult moments. They didn't know I was drinking every night or that I slept with my bedroom light on because I was afraid.

Then one day at work I got an e-mail from one of them. Not just a "Hey, thinking of you" e-mail but pages of chatter. I couldn't believe what I was reading—it was a one way telephone conversation typed in an e-mail. Every few days I received a message, but I never responded to any of them. I kept thinking, *Why doesn't she get it?*

One day, instead of opening the e-mail and reading it, I deleted it. I assumed she would get notices when messages had been opened and read, so there would be no notice for this particular e-mail. That was the last e-mail and contact I had from any of them for months.

I had to park my worry about having hurt their feelings until I had time to deal with it. I already had too much to deal with.

As I sat there on the barstool at night, without the interrupting phone calls, I relived everything that had taken place and the effect it had on everyone. My anger swelled.

Carmon is a general contractor and he worked a few days during the week after Stephanie's funeral. I'm not sure how he was able to do that so soon, but I guess it was better for him to stay busy or at least go through the motions. I was at his home one afternoon when he came in from work. I sat and watched this man who loved his children, had taken care of them, and provided for them. He emptied his lunch cooler and placed it on the small stool that had been Stephanie's when she was a little girl. This hard-working man had probably done this every day for years, part of his routine.

I thought about how I had no children and didn't have a clue what it was to work hard every day to provide for a family. The hardest thing I had to deal with over the most recent years was my nerves when I played the piano in front of people. When I was young and played in the band and at church, I was hardly ever nervous. In recent years, I grew more and more nervous and, as a result, practiced even more to make sure I knew the music almost by memory. Playing the piano had become work. Comparing Carmon's work to mine was a revelation; my work was nothing. I knew then I would not play the piano again. What had I done with my life compared to what he'd done with his? He didn't deserve this. He deserved to have his daughter live, to be able to give her away at her wedding, and to enjoy his grandchildren.

Instead, he had to deal with police and reporters. He had to make multiple trips to Raleigh. One trip was for a press conference at the apartment complex where he had to "make a plea" to the murderer. The police had him say things like, "I want to know my daughter's last words. Did she call out for me before she died?" How excruciating it must have been for him.

Shortly after her death, a memorial scholarship fund was formed to honor Stephanie. Graduating seniors from Franklin County High School who were accepted to Roanoke College could apply and one was selected to receive the scholarship. My sister-in-law told me that when Carmon went to the bank to set up the scholarship account, he couldn't talk—he just started crying. The last time he was in the bank on Stephanie's behalf was when he took her to set up her first checking account.

Not many days after Stephanie's death, Carmon placed a candle in her bedroom window in the front of the house, visible from the highway. He kept a bulb in the candle and never turned it off but always replaced the bulb as soon as it burned out. A news reporter was tearful as they showed a picture of Carmon's home with the candle in the window. To this day people look for the candle and will stop to tell him if they notice it's not burning.

Stephanie's autopsy was released a few weeks after she was murdered. I didn't realize it was common practice to publish autopsies in the local newspaper. Carmon asked the editor to not publish it, but he did not honor Carmon's request. This was one thing he wanted to do to protect his daughter and not have this private information about his child published for everyone to read.

Jay read the autopsy. I didn't think it was a good thing for him to do but where I didn't want to know any more of the bad things that happened, Jay wanted to know everything that happened. I had to be strong when I talked to him on the phone or when we visited on the weekends. Three of his close friends in Virginia came back to California and spent a week with Jay. After they left, he tried to go back to school. He called and wanted my advice on what he should do because one of his classes was about forensic investigations.

"Everything they talk about reminds me of Stephanie and what happened," he said. "It's too hard, Kaye," he started crying.

"You need to do what is healthy for you right now." I said. "You've been though something that not many people have to experience and then to have to be reminded of the bad things every day isn't healthy. You need some time to heal."

Jay spoke with his professors and was excused from classes for the rest of the semester. I grieved for Jay. I knew how I felt and how hard it was for me to deal with everything. It had to be much worse for him.

We were all experiencing "living hell."

I called my mother every Sunday and listened for an hour while she vented and grieved. She always turned the conversation to what Stephanie went through and speculated on what could have happened.

She would say things like, "Do you think he drug her down the hall?" I couldn't deal with these questions but wanted to be supportive. I suggested that she try not to think about those things. Finally, one day she said she had been thinking about talking to a pastor she knew. I encouraged her to do that because after I listened to her every Sunday, I had nightmares. I couldn't do this anymore.

I glanced at the television one night and realized I was looking at the image of a young girl who had been murdered and was lying on a slab in a mortuary. The TV mortician and investigator were casually discussing the victim's demise as the mortician prepared to do an autopsy. My nose started bleeding. That had been Stephanie only a few weeks earlier. I ran to the bathroom, started crying, and shouted out loud, "I hate life. I hate life."

I grieved for Stephanie's boyfriend. This young man was making plans for the rest of his life. He was looking at a house in Charleston, South Carolina, when he got the call from Dee and learned about Stephanie's death. The house could possibly have been where they lived, but now his life and plans to marry Stephanie were shattered.

During his visit to California in August after Stephanie's death, he told me his counselor explained that there was honor in fighting and defending yourself. There must have been something in the news articles, police report, or autopsy, indicating Stephanie had fought. The thick cut in her chin had been an indication.

I knew all too well that we would face another year of firsts. My next trip to Virginia would be my first since she died and she wouldn't be there. Our first Christmas would be unbearable without her, as well as every other holiday, birthday, and milestone event. There would be no wedding to help plan. I would never be able to take her shopping and help buy things for her home. There would be no visit when her first child was born. There would be no grandchildren.

In one of the last e-mails Stephanie sent to me, she suggested that we start a business, a boutique. My response was, "You have the fashion sense, and I'll do the accounting." I thought that when I retired, I would move close to where she lived. I wanted to still be able to spoil her. I wanted to be able to enjoy my niece and eventually, her children.

During one of my visits to Virginia, I spent some time with Jay and Stephanie's friend Jeremy. He told me he slept on the floor at the front door of his house and had a gun next to him in case anyone tried to break in. He was protecting his wife and daughter; Stephanie's murder had driven him to this. He felt responsible because he had recommended that particular apartment complex in Raleigh to Stephanie. I tried to assure him that it wasn't his fault. I repeated what the police psychologist told us.

"The only person responsible for Stephanie's death was the person who broke into her apartment and killed her," I said.

Night after night, I sat on that barstool inside the horseshoe-shaped bar, drank beer, and went through the motions of scrapbooking. Every detail of what we had been through since we learned that she died and more kept going through my mind. The evil man who broke into her apartment and killed her had killed a part of me, too. When Stephanie died, my joy died.

How could it be that the person who did this to my niece and my family be allowed to get up every day, breathe, and go about his life while we had to deal with her death, murder, rape, and watch our loved ones suffer through this madness?

The anger swelled inside me. This anger would be my constant companion until they caught him.

CHAPTER 10
Searching for Answers

———

AFTER WE LOST STEPHANIE, MY trips to Virginia became more frequent. The first time I went home after losing her, I was at Carmon's home visiting with Jennifer and Dee. I couldn't hold back the tears and apologized because I hadn't meant to come to his house and cry. While we were talking, Jennifer mentioned something about God.

"I'm mad at God right now! First Richard and now Stephanie!" I said.

I was mad. I said it like I was mad, and I meant it.

I had been a member of and attended a church in Riverside since 1984 but only attended two or three times from June through December of 2002. The first time I went back to this church, I sat with Vicki near the front about three rows back. As the pastor began his sermon, he came down from the pulpit, walked in my direction, and looked straight at me.

"What do you think goes through someone's mind when they know they're going to die?" he asked.

I stood up and walked out.

This man—my pastor and my friend's husband—had not visited me once since I returned to California. He had shown no concern for my physical, mental, or spiritual wellbeing; I felt I owed him nothing. I had no idea what his sermon was about or his intention by clearly directing that comment at me. It seemed callous, given my circumstances. Returning to this church was not going to help me.

As I spent five months dragging through shock, fear and grief, barely surviving each day, I never once asked God for strength or prayed for anything. I felt that God had abandoned me. Although I knew He hadn't, my communication with Him was nonexistent.

What was the answer to why? Why had this happened to Stephanie? Why did our family have to deal with something like this? Rape and murder happened to other families, not ours. Other families were on the news, not ours!

One night when I was sitting on the barstool drinking a beer, I felt God's presence behind me over my left shoulder. I knew He was there waiting for me, but I was like a child who was mad at a parent, and gave Him the silent treatment.

"I'm not going to pay any attention to You right now. I'm not talking to You," I said.

So He waited.

I had attended church and played the piano or organ for church services for most of my adult life. Some of my most intimate moments with God had been at the piano. I was struggling without my connection to Him and knew I had to reconnect somehow. I had to give in and talk to Him, but when I did, it was more like a confrontation than a conversation.

That night, God waited for me. I was sitting on the barstool, surrounded by scrapbook paraphernalia and pictures, beer in hand, and I finally acknowledged God behind my left shoulder. I slammed my fist down on the granite countertop and shouted out loud.

"Where were You?"

"Where were You when one young girl needed You?"

"Where were Your ten thousand angels that could have protected her?"

"I've loved You all of my life."

"I believe You can do anything."

"Where were You?"

And then I cried.

I didn't get any immediate answers from Him, but from that moment on I started to heal. I stopped drinking beer and started trying to find answers.

I bought the book *The Purpose Driven Life* by Rick Warren. The inside flap of the dust cover states, "This book will help you understand why you are alive and God's amazing plan for you—both here and now, and for eternity. Rick Warren will guide you through a personal *40-day spiritual journey* that will transform your answer to life's most important question: *What on earth am I here for?*"

"Okay, Rick, I'm ready for this. Give me some answers."

The book was designed for a forty-day journey, but I needed and wanted answers now. My brother died, and my niece was murdered. So what's my purpose? What's the purpose of somebody who had to suffer this kind of loss and grief? What on earth was I here for? I didn't want to spend forty days trying to find answers, so I read the book at a fast-forward pace slowing down on specific sections I thought would help me.

I read thirty-three books when I wanted to learn how to manage people and sometimes only learned one thing from each book, so I knew from experience that when I read *The Purpose Driven Life,* I wouldn't be able to turn to a page and see Rick Warren's answer as to why I had to lose my brother or why my niece was murdered, but I had to start somewhere. One message stood out that helped me reconcile my anger toward God:

"Can God handle that kind of frank, intense honesty from you? Absolutely! Genuine friendship is built on disclosure. What may appear as audacity God views as authenticity. God listens to the passionate words of His friends; He is bored with predictable, pious cliches. To be God's friend, you must be honest to God, sharing your true feelings, not what you think you ought to feel or say."[i]

Rick Warren was right. Even though I was yelling at the time, I talked to God with intense honestly. How much closer can you be with someone?

While I was looking for answers as to why, I also started trying to solve a crime. It was always my habit to keep my TV on for company, for friendly noise. During the previous six months, I sat on the bar stool or lay on the couch, existing for a couple of hours before bedtime and all weekend as well with the friendly noise of the TV in the background. Now I was watching TV. I spent every night surfing through the channels looking for crime shows.

Right after the murder, news reporters started calling Carmon. CNN was the first. He declined the interview because it was too soon, only hours after her death. Once he was able to deal with them, he granted interviews to reporters local to Roanoke, Virginia, and Raleigh, North Carolina. I continually searched the channels looking for news articles about Stephanie, but there was never anything on national news. Maybe if CNN had gotten that early interview it would have been on national TV. I'm assuming they wanted "the scoop" on the murder, because they did not ask twice. My thought was that if it had been on national news, more people would have known about it and the guy would have been caught quicker.

One night I thought I finally saw something that would be helpful to the investigation. I was watching a true crime show about a serial killer. The police had pictures of the six women he had murdered on a crime board. I had the sudden realization that they all had dark hair; not one was blond. Stephanie had dark hair. Was this something important? The next day a friend at work reminded me that adult blonds often had dark hair that was dyed blond. I was grasping at a straw.

It seemed like the police were getting nowhere. What had they been doing? Did they have a plain-clothes detective monitoring the people who came to the visitation at the funeral home? Were they videoing it? Did they video the graveside service? Doesn't the person who committed the crime want to be involved in these things and watch people suffer from their handiwork? When Stephanie drove from Raleigh to Rocky Mount, there was a gas station where she always stopped if she needed gas. Did they perform DNA tests on the people who worked there? What about the people she worked with—any DNA tests on them? Are they doing DNA tests on every male within a ten-mile radius of her apartment?

Carmon said yes, they were taking DNA samples. There had been a large number of construction workers at the apartment complex, and it took time to test everyone who had worked there as well as the men who lived there. What if someone refused? Wouldn't that be a clear indicator the person could be a suspect? He told me that of all the people who had been asked for a DNA sample, no one refused. The DNA samples had to be sent to Florida for testing, and it took time. Seriously, Raleigh can't process DNA samples? So if there was a match, couldn't the guy could be long gone before he was apprehended?

During the same week of the interviews with the family members, Dee went to Raleigh to walk through the apartment to help the police with their investigation. Stephanie's stereo and a couple of other things were missing. At one point the police wanted to release this information but needed a picture of the stereo and a description they could use in a news release. Hopefully someone would recognize it and be able to provide information that would lead to an arrest.

Now we had something to do to help with the investigation. The stereo had been a Christmas present years ago from one of her mother's friends. Had anyone taken a picture of Stephanie with the stereo? No. But leave it to my extremely organized nephew—he had the gift receipt that was given to her at the time, and this gave us something to go on. The manufacturer's internet records didn't go back far enough, so we reached out directly to the manufacturer, to no avail. Finally, a friend I worked with was able to get the information we needed to forward to the Raleigh police. Within a few days there was a news article on the Internet showing the picture of the stereo and the data describing it.

Were there any leads as a result of our intense efforts to get the information? None. Well, for a few days anyway, we were extremely hopeful.

The police wanted to announce that a reward was being offered to anyone who could provide information leading to the arrest and conviction of the murderer. There was a press conference in front of Carmon's home; news media vans taped it for the evening news. We were anxious to do this sooner, but the police wanted to wait and announce the reward within the timing of their investigation. We were hopeful and thought surely the one hundred thousand dollar reward that my boss offered would quickly lead to an arrest and conviction, but once again, nothing.

The problem with trying to solve a crime by watching true crime and investigative television shows was that the TV crime was solved in sixty minutes or less. Detectives found answers quickly, and DNA tests were immediate.

In real life, you had to be patient and possibly realize that this crime, so personal and important in your life, might never be solved.

CHAPTER 11

Our Christmas
from Hell

———

In October, I called Delta airlines to get flights for Jay and me to fly home for Christmas. I used frequent flyer miles when I could, and one ticket cost twenty-five thousand points. I was surprised when I saw that I didn't have enough frequent flyer miles. I reviewed the history on my account and discovered that my friends didn't pay for their flights to Virginia when they came for Stephanie's funeral. They used my frequent flyer miles and paid for all of their flights at full price, fifty thousand points each. They used two hundred thousand of my frequent flyer miles and didn't tell me about it or even ask if it was okay.

Shortly thereafter, I attended the church in Riverside, and an elderly man met me at the back door as I was entering. Instead of greeting me or offering his sympathy, he said, "Wasn't it special that those girls went to Virginia?" I smiled and said, "Yes," and at the same time thought that if I'd had enough frequent flyer miles, he could have come, too! I couldn't deal with these friends or their actions, so I buried my feelings about all of it.

I had to pay for Jay's flight and mine to go home for Christmas that year.

In years past, my mother decorated our home and it always resembled a Norman Rockwell Christmas painting. Regardless of what our family was going through at the time, she always made sure our Christmas was as close to normal as possible. The only exception was the year my dad was hospitalized with viral pneumonia. There were no decorations or Christmas Eve dinner that year.

Our first year without Stephanie was no exception for my mother. Ever since Stephanie was a little girl, she helped my mother decorate for Christmas. I don't know how she did it, but my mom decorated our home in honor of Stephanie, and no one would have been able to guess that we were experiencing the worst Christmas of our lives, our Christmas from hell.

Our Christmas Eve tradition had been to clear the dinner table and leave the dishes until later. We went into the living room, and the youngest family member, who for almost twenty years had been Stephanie, passed out the presents. On Christmas Day morning we went to Carmon's to see their gifts and have breakfast before Jay and Stephanie left to go to their mother's.

No one in our family looked forward to Christmas that year. Thinking about any part of it was difficult. As the day approached, it grew more stressful. I just wanted it to be over, for all of us. I worried that none of us would survive it. I don't even remember buying presents.

This would be the first year that Jay, Stephanie, and I did not go Christmas shopping together. Stephanie and I would not sit in the middle of my bedroom floor and wrap presents. None of us would experience the joy of watching Stephanie's excitement.

Dee, Jennifer and I went to the mall one afternoon. Someone had recommended a book for Dee to read and she wanted to give it to me for Christmas, but wanted to tell me about it first and make sure I was okay with it. We went in the book store and she showed me *The Lovely Bones*, a book about a 14-year-old girl who was murdered. If Dee wanted me to have this book, I would accept it. Everyone has to grieve in their own way. If reading this book helped Dee, if giving it to me helped her, I wanted to read it in case she wanted to discuss it later.

The opening sentence of the first chapter read, "My name was Salmon, like the fish; first name, Susie. I was fourteen when I was murdered on December 6, 1973."[ii]

I cringed and closed the book. If I changed a few words, it would read:

"My name was Bennett, originating from the Latin *benedictus*, meaning blessed; first name, Stephanie. I was twenty-three when I was murdered on May 21, 2002."

I would read the book, just not right now.

As a family, we were trying to do things that were different, things that would be a distraction. Carmon's wife, Jennifer, bought a puppy for him. He didn't want the dog but took care of it for a few days before he found a good home for it. We bought a goldfish for my mom, a hopeful distraction for her.

Three of Stephanie's friends came by Carmon's when we were getting the goldfish bowl ready. They had been going to businesses around Rocky Mount dressed in Christmas outfits, performing a dance routine for a donation to Stephanie's Memorial Scholarship Fund. They wanted to perform their dance for Carmon before they gave him the money they had collected. When they started dancing, I started crying. It was just heart breaking.

"It's not fair is it?" Jennifer said.

I couldn't say anything. I just shook my head in agreement.

These were some of Stephanie's closest friends. She should have been with them.

It was Christmas Eve. My mom prepared the meal and we asked her to not serve the food. Carmon, Jennifer, Jay, and Dee came to my mom's. Carmon sat at the bar between the kitchen and dining room and Jay sat across from him. Watching Carmon, who had lost his daughter, and Jay, who had lost his sister, was distressing. Carmon's facial expression and body language was that of someone doing their best to keep it together and not totally break down. His stress seemed immeasurable. I wanted Christmas to be over for him.

Jay wanted Carmon to have a moment of joy before dinner. He asked his dad to open one of his gifts, a camera that we bought for him, because Carmon liked to take pictures. The gift provided only the slightest moment of joy.

We just talked in spurts for a little while, about nothing really. We didn't know what to say. The tension was broken when my mom's boss and his wife stopped by to bring her a gift. He briefly asked Carmon about the investigation before they left.

When it was time for dinner, we couldn't sit at the table as a family like we'd done for so many years. One by one we took our plates, went into the kitchen to serve ourselves. Carmon and Jay ate at the bar and the rest of us sat randomly at the table. We didn't go into the living room after dinner where the Christmas tree was or exchange gifts that evening.

When Jay left that night, he cried when he asked us to not come to Carmon's on Christmas morning. We assured him that we would wait until the afternoon. We went the next day, but Jay didn't come. Coming back to Carmon's that afternoon, his and Stephanie's tradition for many years, was too hard for him.

Jennifer told us that Dee got up late on Christmas morning and it took her a long time to open her presents. She would open one, cry and wait a while before opening another one.

Finally, Christmas was over. I was so relieved. We survived it and wouldn't have to think about it or worry about it for another year.

Many tears were shed that year. I was so proud of my family and the way we navigated an extremely difficult Christmas by loving, caring, and supporting each other. We followed each other's lead as we individually, but together, made our way through the traditions we could endure.

When I returned to California after Christmas, I stopped sleeping with my light on. My mother lived alone and didn't sleep with her light on. I decided that if she could do it, I could do it, even if I was still afraid. I finally figured out what to do about my fear and laid an open Bible next to me on the bed so the word of God would be open to the darkness of my bedroom. I spoke out loud in my bedroom the first night I opened my Bible and turned the light off.

"In the name of Jesus Christ, stay out of my house and stay out of my head," I spoke to evil.

There is power in the name of Jesus, and I depended on that power to keep evil away. Since then, I have not been afraid and my Bible is still laying open on my nightstand.

CHAPTER 12

A New Church Home

VENTURING OUTSIDE OF MY HOUSE for something other than work was hard for me; I had become a recluse. In March of the next year, I still hadn't attended church or made any attempts to find a new church home. Easter was in April, and I knew I could not stay at home on Easter Sunday, so I decided to visit Crossroads Church in Corona. I went on the Sunday before Easter to check things out, find where to park, and know where to go when I returned for the Easter service. I had not thought beyond Easter.

The best part about attending a different church would be that no one would know me or what I was dealing with. I didn't have to talk to anyone, answer any questions, or suffer knowing looks from people who knew my situation.

I arrived at Crossroads, walked from the parking lot to the "Plex" a small auditorium and ignored the greeter who was trying to make eye contact with me. I'd felt fortunate that I found an aisle seat. I sat through the entire service willing myself not to cry. There were moments when I did but kept it together for the most part. Every time I saw a young girl my thoughts went to Stephanie and how I used to have her in my life. I experienced those feelings whenever I attended church for quite some time.

Barry McMurtrie, the senior pastor, was probably in his late fifties. He spoke with an Australian accent and had a warmth about him that made me feel instantly comfortable and welcome. I sat through the service, not really listening to much of anything except when he announced the sermon series he intended to start the Sunday after Easter. It would address why God allowed bad things to happen. I knew then I was in the right place; this is where God wanted me to be. Every Sunday I parked in the same place, sat in the same general area, spoke to no one, and left immediately when the service was over.

I was still trying to solve the crime, obsessed with the fact that the person who murdered my niece was able to get up every day, breathe, and go about his normal life. I couldn't and wouldn't talk to people about what was going on in my life, so I became a recluse at church in the midst of thousands of people. Even after the construction was complete on a larger auditorium and we started having services there, I found an aisle seat far to the right, up about eighteen steps where the lighting was dim every Sunday. After the service, I could leave through the side door and make it to my car without coming in contact with anyone.

The church services I grew up in and the ones I had experienced to this point in my life were traditionally structured. Not to say that a contemporary service doesn't have structure, but it's a more relaxed atmosphere. It's okay to dress casual or bring your coffee in with you to drink during the service. In a traditional service there are usually two Bible verses—one from the Old Testament and one from the New Testament. At Crossroads, a sheet was provided each Sunday with an outline of the message, listing multiple Bible verses that would be referenced with room for notes.

I also noticed that nearly everyone carried their Bibles to church. At the Methodist church I was raised in and the Christian church

I used to attend, hardly anyone brought their Bibles to church, including me (I was always carrying music). Maybe they weren't necessary if there's only going to be two or three Bible verses used for the entire message. At Crossroads, whenever a Bible verse was referenced, everyone started turning the pages of their Bibles. Someone once said that hearing the turning of hundreds of Bible pages all at once was like listening to holy rain.

The Sunday evening service was more like a Bible study. I started attending and for several years went to both services on Sundays. I sat in the same seat and had little to no contact with anyone.

Every now and then I ran into someone I knew at the grocery store. A friend/neighbor asked where I was going to church, and I told him Crossroads in Corona. He said that he'd heard of the church and that it was a "feel good" church—meaning they wanted everyone to feel good when they left. I didn't quite know what he meant; it sounded negative. Of course I felt good when I left; feeling good for me meant something totally different than what he was referring to, I'm sure. I felt good simply because I was attending church again.

One Sunday during the service, Pastor Barry repeated the same thing in his message—that people referred to Crossroads as a "feel good" church. His response was, "Who wants to go to church and leave feeling bad?" I agreed with Pastor Barry. For the first time in a year, I enjoyed going to church, I learned a lot about the Bible, more so than ever before, and I looked forward to it every Sunday.

When I was in my early twenties, I purchased a new Bible, *The Way, The Living Bible*, which was designed with young adults in mind. The book itself was green, a six-by-nine paperback. The illustrations had pictures of young adults, and there was a brief description in front of each book that a young adult could easily understand. Most importantly for me, it was written in modern-day English instead of the King James Version, which also helped.

This Bible also featured a chart of the books of the Bible, listed down the left side of the page. The rest of the page was filled with a grid of checkboxes. Each book had numbered boxes next to the name of the book corresponding to the number of chapters in the book. My goal had been to read the entire Bible and check the boxes as I read the chapters to mark my progress. Even though I kept this Bible close to me all the time, I had, at some point, stopped reading it.

Now that I attended this "feel good" church and was mentally returning to life, I felt motivated to finish reading my Bible. I started reading it on August 21, 1974. I finally finished and wrote the date August 20, 2004. I'm ashamed to say it took me thirty years to read the entire Bible. Had I read this Bible so I could draw closer to God and understand His Word? No, but all of the numbered boxes were checked!

One Sunday afternoon, I sat in my family room with the gas fireplace on, and I was trying to decide which book to read on this rainy, cold, wrap-in-a-blanket and read-a-good-book kind of day. I had a bookcase full of books I'd read and a few small stacks yet to read. I realized if anyone came into my home and saw all the books, there was little evidence that I was a Christian. Ninety percent of my bookcase was filled with secular books. I had one small section of hymnbooks, a Bible dictionary, and a parallel New Testament.

My thoughts turned to the Bible.

Crossroads started a daily Bible reading plan in January, so I decided to get the reading plan out, catch up to February, and make that my goal for the year—no checkboxes required. Following this reading plan would take me through the Old Testament once and the New Testament twice. This time I read the New American Standard version with large print.

Now I had a new goal; not only to read the Bible using this reading plan but also to study it and know it. I had been a Christian all of my life, but I would be in conversations when something in the Bible would be referenced and they would say, "You know, Kaye…" I would look at them blankly and nod my head. They didn't know that I didn't know.

The best way for me to learn was to take notes, write them down, and then study them. I purchased a ruled composition book with a black and white hard cover. I covered the front and back of the notebook with scrapbook paper. Then I took a six-by-nine mailing envelope, cut and folded it to make a pocket of sorts, and glued it inside the back cover. This is where I kept the handouts from the church services. And so began my journaling.

I had never been interested in journaling before. But now with my new goal and my self-designed notebook, I eagerly made notes every day, my own special version of journaling. When I read Exodus about the specifics of the construction of the arc of the covenant, I found a picture of it on the Internet, printed it and pasted it in my journal. I referred to the picture as I read the instructions God gave to the people of Israel on how to build it. If I came across a word I didn't understand, I looked up the definition and wrote it in my journal.

My page on *hyssop* looks something like this:

Hyssop has been used for millennia as a holy herb, consecrated for cleaning holy places. Hyssop is an evergreen bushy herb growing one-to two-feet high on a square stem with linear leaves and flowers in whorls of six to-fifteen blooms.

Exodus 12:22: "You shall take a bunch of hyssop and dip it in the blood which is in the basin, and apply some of the blood that is in the basin to the lintel and the two doorposts; and none of you shall go outside the door of his house until morning."

I searched hyssop on the Internet to see exactly what it looked like, and I also searched for the definition of *lintel* and noted both in my journal. I wrote specific Bible verses that stood out to me, sometimes even entire chapters. I also incorporated notes from the Sunday services.

I was well into my journaling and had filled about two-thirds of my journal when the thought that kept entering into my mind was to write down the bold headings that are before the chapters and sometimes within the chapters of Job. That seemed like a lot of work, so I wouldn't do it. Then the thought would be there again—write down the bold headings that are before the chapters and sometimes within the chapters of Job. The book of Job is full of Job grieving, his friends talking, Job talking, and God talking to Job, which all can be confusing. Still, I didn't write them down.

I ignored these thoughts until one Sunday afternoon they were there again, so I gave in and said, "Okay, I will write them down." Perhaps by doing so I would understand the book of Job better. So I opened my journal and made sure I had two blank pages. I wanted to start at the top of the left page and finish at the bottom of the right page. (My spiritual gift is organization.)

Job has forty-two chapters. It worked out perfect with twenty-one chapters per page.

"God Displeased with Job's Friends" was the next-to-last bold heading in the book of Job. The moment I saw it, I realized He was displeased with my friends as well. I highlighted this heading in my journal. From that moment on, I did not feel bad about the way things turned out when my friends attended Stephanie's funeral, when they called so often and didn't give me the alone time I needed, and when I learned they used all of my frequent flyer miles. The feelings I had were gone. God had been telling me to write these headings down, and I hadn't listened. He wanted me to stop feeling bad about what happened; He knew I already had enough to deal with. I kept a white ribbon in my journal where my Job pages were to remind me that God helped me and that I needed to listen to Him.

Months later, I ran into one of these friends at a CVS Pharmacy one night after work. Our greeting was like one of old friends. She asked if I was attending church and where.

"Crossroads, and the best thing about it is…" I said.

"No one knows," she finished the sentence for me. She understood; no one at Crossroads knew what I was going through.

I like to think that God orchestrated our meeting as well.

Another method I used to learn the Bible was to rent biblical movies. I read the Bible concerning the character, watched the movie, and then watched the movie and simultaneously read the Bible, marking specific verses that followed the story in the movie. For example, I read the Book of Acts a couple of times and then watched the movie *Paul the Apostle.* Then I watched the movie on my laptop, had my Bible in front of me, and followed the story in my Bible as the movie played. I did this a couple of times and afterward felt I knew Paul like a friend. In the last scene of the movie, as Paul turned toward Rome, I wanted to say, "Paul, don't go to Rome!"

Not all movies follow the story as well as I thought they should; they took liberties and tried to fill in the blanks. Hopefully God had His hands in the making of these movies and we could trust the contents. The movies I found helpful were:

Samson and Delilah : Biography
One Night with the King
Jeremiah
Paul the Apostle
King David
The Story of Jacob and Joseph
The Nativity Story
Joseph and the Amazing Technicolor Dreamcoat

Joseph and the Amazing Technicolor Dreamcoat was a Broadway musical by Andrew Lloyd Weber. I recommended this play to a friend, and she left during the intermission; she found it to be "not spiritual." I loved the music and, yes, it didn't come across as a spiritual play, but it did impress the story of Joseph in my mind and helped me remember the details of his story. I could understand what she meant, because when I saw *Jesus Christ, Superstar*, another Andrew Lloyd Weber musical, I felt like I should not be watching such a sacrilegious play. Needless to say *Jesus Christ, Superstar* did not make my list.

Studying and journaling had increased my knowledge of the Bible to the point where I felt comfortable being involved in discussions. It was a good start for my goal to learn and know the Bible.

CHAPTER 13
Some Good News

————————

JAY GRADUATED THOMAS JEFFERSON SCHOOL of Law in May 2004, two years after we lost Stephanie. Carmon, Jennifer, Dee, Stephanie's boyfriend, and Jay's friend Bradley flew from Virginia and stayed at my house along with Jennifer's brother Kevin and his wife. Everyone arrived a couple of days early to make a small vacation out of it. Jay and his girlfriend came from San Diego. My mom arrived two days later.

The graduation services were held at Spreckels Organ Pavilion in Balboa Park. Jay walked across the stage that day and received his Juris Doctorate. We were so proud of him and celebrated at dinner that night. Three of Jay's friends joined us; two of them flew from Virginia and the third from Texas.

The only person missing was Stephanie and we had a few tearful moments because of it.

A few days later, Bradley and Jay left California, driving to Virginia. Jay was moving home.

Although it hadn't seemed possible at the time of Stephanie's death, we were actually doing better; everyone that is, except Jay.

Jay also had a problem with alcohol, although I never really knew the severity of it. After he moved to San Diego to study law, I was excited to have him so close and be around him more, but I began to see and experience things firsthand. Like college, it took him longer to graduate from law school than it should have. I attributed it to his alcohol consumption, but the loss of his sister and also the loss of one of his friends took their toll on him.

Jay kept it together long enough to graduate from law school, but when he moved back to Virginia, alcoholism, grief, and depression took over. Depression comes easy when you're dealing with grief and murder. Alcohol breeds depression and depression breeds alcohol; it was a vicious cycle that disabled him. His girlfriend of three years broke up with him and that added to his grief and depression. Jay and I talked often and I worried about him. It took years for me to deal with Richard's death, and I worried that Jay would suffer even longer because of the way we lost Stephanie.

Next year, in the summer of 2005, Tina, one of Stephanie's friends, had a destination wedding on the beach in Santa Barbara, California. Dee and Martha, another one of Stephanie's close friends, were going to be in the wedding, and I was also invited. They came a few days early and stayed with me. It was the first time they'd visited since we'd lost Stephanie. Both of these girls had been to California with her when she spent a week with me. It was a difficult few days for us because Stephanie should have been there, too.

We drove to Santa Barbara in time for the girls to go to the rehearsal. I met them at the dinner, which was extremely hard to sit through. Some of Stephanie's closest friends were there, but she wasn't. I cried through most of the dinner. It just wasn't fair that we didn't have her.

The next day an arch was erected on the beach for the wedding party to stand before. Guests sat in white chairs. I walked onto the beach and took a seat on the bride's side a few rows back. The wedding started, and from that moment on it was difficult to not cry.

I was grateful for my prescription sunglasses; no one could see my eyes and the tears.

Part of the service was to acknowledge the yellow rose in the girls' bouquets put there in memory of Stephanie. There was also another flower in memory of the bride's teenage cousin who had recently passed from leukemia. Three candles in glass containers were also lit in memory of the bride and groom's grandparents, Stephanie, and the bride's cousin. That's all it took for me, and I was an official mess. At one point Dee looked at me. She told me later that she had looked to me for encouragement but saw I would be no help.

At the receptions in Santa Barbara and later in Rocky Mount, Stephanie was remembered. At one point during each of the receptions, the DJ announced, "This one's for you, Steph." He played "Dixieland Delight" by Alabama. Stephanie's friends formed a circle on the dance floor surrounding the bride and groom. As soon as the song began, the DJ joined the circle and everyone started dancing to the music. They went through the steps of a routine that Stephanie and one of her friends had choreographed for the song. It was clear that her friends were not strangers to this song or the dance.

Three months later, on October 19, 2005 three and one half years after Stephanie's death, I was sitting at my desk at the end of the work day when my phone rang. I saw that it was Carmon and told my friend Dave, who was sitting at my desk, that I needed to answer it.

"Are you ready for some good news?" he asked.

"I don't know. It depends on what it is," I said.

"The Raleigh police have made an arrest, and it's a positive DNA match," he said.

It took a second for me to wrap my mind around what he said. *Wow! This has actually happened.* It was surreal.

I had waited so long for this phone call that I had almost given up on it ever happening and got to the point of not thinking about it every day. I still had a hard time dealing with the fact that the person who murdered Stephanie could get up every day, breathe, and go about his life as usual. But now it was over. Finally, he would not be able to go about his life as usual, although he could still breathe.

"Who was it? Does Dee know him?" I asked.

"No, Dee doesn't know him."

His name was Drew Planten, a chemist who worked for the State of North Carolina and lived in the apartment complex next to Stephanie and Dee. His supervisor was working with the Raleigh police and tried twice to get a DNA sample. The first time was when she had an ice cream social for some of her employees. The plan was to get a DNA sample from his drinking glass or the silverware he used, but when he left the restaurant that day, Planten wiped his glass clean and took the silverware with him. The second time was when she had Planten redo a test of something he had worked on, but that time she had him wear gloves. When the test was complete, she asked him for the gloves. His hands were shaking when he handed them to her. She gave them to the police, and the DNA test was processed immediately. It was the positive match.

Planten was arrested as he left work. The police were waiting for him when he opened the door of the building to leave. They apprehended him and forced him to the ground. Because he had a gun concealed in the jacket he was wearing, the police told Carmon that he would probably have killed himself or caused himself to be killed during the arrest if he had the chance.

How ironic that Dave, my friend and co-worker who helped me the day when I learned of Stephanie's death, was sitting in my office when Carmon called to tell me about the arrest. When Dave realized who I was talking to and what my conversation was about, he got up to leave. I motioned for him to stay seated, but he didn't. I assumed he thought I would be upset and needed privacy. I was neither upset nor did I cry. This was definitely good news.

There were two close friends I wanted to share this information with, and I called them as soon as my conversation with Carmon ended. Their responses were the same as mine: "Wow," and then silence. I called Jay and my mom. Carmon had told them prior to calling me and they already had some time to absorb it. Jay felt the same way I did: it was surreal. I could tell my mother felt the same way but she couldn't put it into words. Instead, she called him that "mean old man."

I felt as if a burden had been lifted from my life. I was ready to talk to people about what had happened. I wanted to share this good news.

At the end of every church service, Pastor Barry asked anyone with a joy or concern to share it with him. Besides my two friends, he was the first person I told outside of work. After the next Sunday morning service, I approached him and told him my joy.

"My niece was murdered three-and-a-half years ago, and just this week they arrested the person who did it, and the DNA was a positive match," I said.

For an instant his face was unreadable. I guess he wasn't expecting to hear a joy like mine.

"God bless you," he said after a moment.

During the next appointment with my hairdresser, Liz, I told her my story. I also told her that my first venture outside of my house after Stephanie's death, other than work, was to an appointment with her. I had sat through that appointment hardly saying a word. I remember sitting under the dryer, my highlights heating, while I read an article about the Green River Killer, a serial killer in Washington State. It seemed that murder was everywhere.

I thanked her for giving me the space I so badly needed back then and not chatting away like a lot of people would have done. It was almost like she could sense I needed the quiet. She couldn't believe that I'd not shared any of this over the last three years.

I felt comfortable sharing my story with two other friends. One was the lady who had helped me at Nordstrom for several years, and a customer at work who came in my office periodically. Everyone had a different reaction. Sometimes I was asked if we knew where Stephanie had been taken, and that surprised me. I had to explain that she hadn't been kidnapped.

The crime had been solved, and I didn't need to search crime shows or watch the news anymore. I haven't watched another crime show to this day. Before we lost Stephanie, I used to watch those shows for enjoyment. I thought they were interesting, but when murder hits home, they're not interesting anymore. People watch the nightly news and there's always something about a murder, a kidnapping accompanied by murder, an abduction, or abuse. It's news. When this type of thing actually occurs in your life, it's not news. It's reality. Evil has crept into your life and destroyed someone close and dear to you.

The news of the arrest was the final rock thrown into the peaceful lake our lives had become. The rippling effect of evil resurfaced.

Although the news was good for our family, it was still upsetting. It brought back all the memories of what happened to Stephanie. We had finally reached a new level of normal, and those feelings from three and a half years ago were fresh again. Carmon had to endure more interviews for the media. The Internet had frequent, almost daily, news articles revisiting the crime and reporting about the arrest.

Carmon and Jennifer had to go to Raleigh to look at things found in his apartment, some of which may have belonged to Stephanie. They identified her laundry basket and the stereo. Other items found lead to the solving of another case: a cold case in Michigan that happened a few years prior to Stephanie's death. A girl had been shot in the face getting out of her car when she arrived home from work one night. I was glad that her family finally had an answer to who murdered their daughter.

Other things provided proof he was stalking another young girl. Only God knows how many people this man had murdered. When I'm asked if anything good came out of Stephanie's murder, I tell people about the crime that was solved and the one that was prevented.

As evidenced by the picture on the Internet, Drew Planten was dressed in an orange and white striped prison uniform and strapped to a wheelchair when he was brought into the courtroom for his arraignment. He would not hold his head up or speak. From my understanding, he was being held in solitary confinement.

The news of the arrest made everything fresh again for Jay and it was hard for him. He was still in the never-ending cycle of grief, depression, and alcohol. We made plans for him to move back to California after Christmas to live and work with me. I left two days after Christmas and Jay left a couple of days later. On his way to California, he had to change planes in Atlanta. It was during this layover that he called.

"I wanted to let you know that I'm in an ambulance on the way to a hospital in Atlanta," he said. "The plane was taxiing out to the runway and the passengers seated near me said I had a seizure."

"Are they sure it was a seizure?" I asked.

"That's what they said."

"How do you feel?"

20

"I feel fine."

"Could it be an allergic reaction to something? Did you eat anything different today?"

"No, nothing."

He was as surprised as I was. I talked to him several times that afternoon, and each time he sounded progressively worse. I could tell something was wrong by his sometimes incoherent and slurred speech. I booked a flight to Atlanta.

The next two days were eye opening for me as I experienced his detox. When I arrived at the hospital, I told the nurses I would take care of him. I closed the door to his hospital room and spent the rest of that day, night, and the next day caring for him.

"You will be blessed for taking such good care of him," a nurse said. "Get him away from where he came from, away from the people he was drinking with, and don't let him go back."

Jay had been drinking heavily and stopped in preparation of coming to California, and because of it, had an alcoholic seizure. He didn't remember anything about the two sleepless nights, the hallucinations, or anything else during the time he paced the room. It hurt to see him suffer through detoxing.

Carmon arrived from Virginian on day two of Jay's hospitalization. The next day, the doctor was in with Jay; I was sitting on a couch in a waiting area in the hospital when Carmon approached me. I was exhausted but turned my head to look at him.

"I just talked to the Raleigh police," he said. "Drew Planten hung himself in his jail cell."

It was January 3, 2006, approximately two months after the arrest.

I turned my head back and stared into the space in front of me. I didn't say anything for a minute, but then I said, "Good!"

This man could no longer breathe, and our family would be saved the ordeal of a trial. We would not have to sit and listen to the gruesome details of how he stalked her, how he attacked her, or what Stephanie went through the night she was murdered. When I think of other families who had to deal with a trial in highly-publicized murder cases, I can't imagine how they endured it. Thankfully, our ordeal was over.

I was the only member of my family who felt this way. Others wanted to be able to confront him. *Why Stephanie?*

My response to this was, "Do you think he would look at you, answer any questions, or even speak? He had to be strapped to a chair and wheeled into the courtroom for his arraignment."

Why Stephanie? Because he could!

We sat in Jay's hospital room together and watched the news.

"That guy ruined my life," Jay said.

That guy ruined all of our lives.

Before we left the hospital, I told Jay what I expected him to do. *You will attend church with me every Sunday. You will go to Celebrate Recovery on Friday nights. You will go to AA. You will not have alcohol in my house.* Jay and I had always been close, and I thought our relationship would overpower the problem with alcohol, but I was foolish. Alcoholism told him, "You don't have to go to church, you don't have to go to Celebrate Recovery, you don't have to go to AA, and it's okay to bring alcohol into the house."

I hoped that moving back to California and living with me would get him away from his drinking buddies and give him a new start. Unfortunately, no matter where you go, alcoholism goes with you. I like to think the rules I gave Jay lasted for a few days at least, but he didn't follow them.

I shared with Jay how my dad's drinking caused his personality to change toward my mother, what our weekends were like growing up, and how I always tried to protect Richard from my dad's outbursts. We had some really good conversations, but conversations don't cure alcoholism.

We were trying to get used to living with each other. I had lived alone for many years and because of his depression and drinking for the last year and a half, he wasn't used to a structured life. He didn't have a driver's license so he had to depend on me for transportation. It seemed like I was always running late for work, a lifetime issue, and Jay was annoyed that he always had to wait for me in the morning. He didn't like being late for work, not even one minute.

We had some issues every now and then, but navigated our way through them. It was an adjustment for both of us.

CHAPTER 14
Alcoholism Is a Thief

———

JAY WAS STILL GRIEVING STEPHANIE. On our way to work one morning, he asked, "How did you do it when Richard died?"

"It took eight years, and what worked for me was being able to talk about it to someone who actually listened to what I was saying. If anybody tries to tell you that you should be over it, don't listen to them. You're the only person who was Stephanie's brother; no one knows what you're feeling except you. People don't know what it's like. Most people your age haven't experienced anything like this. They especially don't know what it's like to deal with murder," I said. "I know it doesn't seem like it now, but it will get better."

We had many good days, but as much as I loved Jay, it was hard for me to have someone in my home all the time after living alone for many years. It was hard for Jay as well. One Saturday night he went out and didn't come home until noon the next day. I confronted him about it, explaining that what happened to Stephanie made me fear for his safety. I had expected the worse, that he would not be sober, but he was.

We had a few rough moments, all of which I attribute to alcoholism and the addictive personality I didn't understand.

"Do you think I want to be like this? Why can't I be like everybody else?" Jay asked me when he was detoxing after a relapse.

I knew he meant it. He was handsome, smart, and had so much potential. He wanted a normal life, but alcoholism was stealing it from him.

Early one morning, Jay handed me his insurance card, told me he wanted to go to rehab, and then went back to his room. This was what I'd been waiting for. I reached for the telephone and called Carmon to let him know and then called two or three different rehab facilities, Betty Ford being the last one. He had a ten minute telephone interview with them. There was space available, and later that morning we drove to the city of Rancho Mirage, and he was admitted.

A nurse took him to a detox facility while a counselor talked to me. I answered the questions, filled out the paperwork, and waited while they charged my credit card. I explained that Jay had always had a problem with alcohol, gave the counselor a little of his history—what I knew of it anyway—and explained that he had maintained until he graduated from law school but after that went off the deep end. I explained that his sister had been raped and murdered by a serial killer and that had escalated the plunge. I asked if they could help him.

I recognized the familiar expression on the counselor's face and could tell he was thinking, *Wow.*

"You're kidding," he said.

"No. Can you help him with this?" I asked.

"Yes. Did they catch the guy?"

I told him yes, gave him Stephanie's name, explained that it happened in Raleigh and if he wanted to know more about it he could search the Internet. My concern was that they help Jay. I'm sure his concern was for Jay as well, but people are always shocked when they hear of her murder and then they start asking questions.

Jay came back a few minutes later so we could say goodbye and then returned to the detox facility. I walked out to my car, then sat and cried for a long time. As I drove away, I called Carmon to let him know the day's events and asked him to let Jay's mother know.

I was emotionally drained. When I was younger, I used to think that when I reached my fifties I would be enjoying Jay and Stephanie's children. I imagined I would travel to wherever they lived to spend time with them, spoil them, and eventually, when I retired, move close to them. Never did I imagine I would lose Stephanie, much less lose her the way we did, or that I would be taking Jay to the Betty Ford Center to be admitted for treatment. Life didn't seem fair, for any of us.

Carmon called that afternoon to check on me.

"You sound better than you did earlier today when you called," he said.

"Well, after Jay was admitted, I came home and drank a couple glasses of wine and a beer," I said. "Is there something wrong with this picture?"

Before Jay came to live with me, I removed everything from my house that contained alcohol. I gave away bottles of wine and champagne I had received as gifts so when he moved in, there was absolutely no alcohol in my home. I had stopped at a grocery store on the way home from Betty Ford.

Jay wasn't allowed to contact anyone outside of Betty Ford during the first week, but he was granted one phone call to me on Saturday night. He said that when he packed his clothes, he didn't realize how cool it would be in the desert at night. I dropped off warmer clothes at the facility, but I didn't get to see him.

The next week he called to tell me who he met. A celebrity entered the facility under the name of Don Amen.

"I'm sitting here looking straight across the room at "Don Amen," Jay said. "I know it's him because I recognize the tattoo on his arm."

Jay explained that when someone new is admitted to the facility, a resident is asked to meet the person, advise him of the rules, and show him the campus. The administrators asked Jay to greet this newcomer. He and "Don" became close friends.

Carmon came to California, and we went to the Betty Ford Center for family week. We were separated into different groups and spent the next five days learning about alcoholism.

One morning the residents and their family members were in a large meeting room, each with their own group. The counselor who led the meeting that day talked about the role assumed by family members in an alcoholic environment.

The middle child was the lost child.

The middle child was the one who was in the corner protecting and shielding the younger sibling from the effects of alcoholism in the home.

The middle child was the most successful.

The middle child was single.

When the counselor finished, I turned to look at Jay who was on the other side of the room with Carmon. He was looking at me. When we made eye contact, he pointed at me.

Jay knew it and I knew it.

I was the middle child.

I spent most of Richard's life trying to shield him from the effects of alcoholism in our home.

I was the most successful.

I was single for almost all of my life.

I was the lost child.

My dad was an alcoholic, my husband was an alcoholic, and Jay was an alcoholic. Alcoholism had stolen from all of them. I had been around alcoholism and addiction my entire life and although I wasn't an alcoholic, I learned that alcoholism affected my life in ways I never knew before. Alcoholism was a thief; it stole from everyone in many ways.

I felt sad when I imagined what my life might have been like if it hadn't been influenced by alcoholism and addiction. Would I have had a healthy, happy marriage? Would I have had children? Based on the characteristics of the lost child, the chances seemed likely.

Carmon and I met with Jay's counselor that afternoon.

"I have good news, and I have bad news." the counselor said. "The good news is that Jay is extremely smart. The bad news is that he has a high tolerance for alcohol."

The good news also turned out to be bad news. When people with this disease are that intelligent, they usually think they have it all figured out, are smarter than the disease, and can control it. The bad news about a high tolerance for alcohol meant that each time Jay drank, it took more for him to reach the point of stopping.

The counselor explained it this way. Imagine a meter in the shape of a half circle. The first time someone drinks and has two glasses of alcohol, the hand on the meter moves up a fraction of an inch. The next time a person with a high tolerance for alcohol drinks, it takes more than two glasses to get to the same point, and even more to move the hand a fraction higher, and so on. Each time the person drinks, it always takes more to get to the place where they stop, until the hand on the meter is beyond the safe zone and well into the last space on the meter, the red zone. When you drink that much and suddenly stop, you have alcoholic seizures three days later. So having a high tolerance to alcohol was definitely not good news.

I also learned that I was an enabler, because I enabled Jay to persist in self-destructive behavior. I set boundaries when he came to live with me but didn't enforce them. I always gave him money when he asked for it, sometimes even more than he asked for. I nursed him through detox. I paid bills for him instead of saying no and forcing him to get a job to earn money to pay them himself.

It was hard to accept the fact that my helping Jay was hurting him.

The counselor's advice was to allow, even force the alcoholic to fend for himself. They recommended that I not allow Jay to return to my home and continue living with me. I just couldn't do it. It seemed pretty drastic to me to tell my nephew that he didn't have a place to live when he had gone through rehab for help and was ready for a fresh start.

During Jay's second month of rehab, he was moved to a facility in a residential area. The residents were given money each week, and it was their responsibility to buy groceries and cook their meals. When I visited Jay, I took three canned jars of my homemade vegetable beef soup.

Jay shared the soup with his friends.

"The next time people make fun of your cooking, tell them that Don Amen likes your homemade soup," Jay said, teasing me for my lack of culinary abilities.

After two months of rehab, I picked up Jay on a Friday night; being on the freeway for the first time in eight weeks made him feel a little apprehensive. During our ride home, he explained that he thought it was his sobriety that made the sky look bluer, the trees greener, and the air fresher. Jay also told me that Don Amen helped him deal with Stephanie's death. Don must have been the kind of friend who truly listened, and for that, I will always be grateful to him.

One of the things we learned at Betty Ford was that alcoholics hide their alcohol in many places. If their alcohol is discovered in one place, they have backup hidden somewhere else. When Jay was in rehab, I went through everything in his room, trying to find bottles of alcohol. I felt sure that I'd been thorough. However, when I brought Jay home from Betty Ford that night, he went to his bedroom and brought me an empty bottle. He explained that it was there when he left and he hadn't drank anything right then. I was shocked. How could I have possibly missed it?

For the first time in many years, I experienced Jay completely sober. I was amazed at the person he was and told Carmon that I was sorry he wasn't experiencing his son's sobriety.

Christmas was only three weeks away. Jay didn't want to go home for Christmas, and I didn't want him to be alone during the holiday season, so we both stayed in California. I had an artificial ficus tree in the corner of my family room. I decorated it with lights and placed two or three poinsettias at its base. That was our Christmas tree and I even prepared a Christmas dinner for the two of us. In January, Jay stayed at home and studied to take the bar exam.

I would like to say that Jay continued as a recovering alcoholic, but I can't. He relapsed six months later when he learned that he didn't pass the bar exam.

Jay didn't go back to work. Instead he suffered with alcoholism and addiction in my home for the next six months. It wore on me, being at work every day, knowing that he was at my house, drinking and depressed, suffering through this vicious cycle. Every day, every night was the same. He stayed in his room, hardly ever coming out. In December, I finally arranged for Jay to live with my friend, Shane Nerenberg, a pastor, and his wife Jennie.

Shane had started a church and I knew he and his wife would be a good influence for Jay and that he and Jay would become close friends. Shane wasn't much older than Jay and had taken in young men with similar problems, although those young men were placed there by the court. After a few weeks with Shane, Jay got a job in a law firm and moved into an apartment by himself.

I continued to go to church twice on Sunday. Our new Senior Pastor, Chuck Booher, was leading a study on Revelations during the Sunday evening service. He spoke about when he became a Christian and was on fire for Christ. He bought a Living Bible, written in modern day English, and read it, cover to cover, in a matter of weeks.

Wait a minute! As he was describing the Bible he had read, I realized I was holding one just like it in my lap. It was the same Bible I bought as a young adult and marked checkboxes as I read it. He read this Bible in a few weeks. It took me thirty years to read it! Ouch!

Pastor Chuck referenced verses in Revelations about a church who had been on fire, had been filled with burning love for Jesus, whose desire was to emulate Christ, but had forgotten.

"But I have this against you, that you have left your first love. Therefore remember from where you have fallen, and repent and do the deeds you did at first; or else I am coming to you and will remove your lampstand out of its place—unless you repent." *Rev 2:4-5*

Another lesson he taught, was from the Beatitudes.

"Blessed are those who mourn, for they shall be comforted." *Matt 5: 4*

When I read this verse before, I thought it referred to grief. Mourning meant to grieve when someone dies, but we grieved in ways different from the conventional signs or sorrow over a person's death. Pastor Chuck explained that to mourn meant to grieve when we learn what a relationship with Christ truly means, and realize that our relationship hadn't been what it should have been.

And I mourned.

I grieved that I had wavered at times in my life. I wavered when we lost Richard. I told people that life got in the way. I was trying to deal with grief, moved to California, moved back to Virginia, married and divorced someone I was not compatible with. I had not tithed in several years. I found a church home again in Riverside, California, started tithing, played the piano again in Sunday services, but after we lost Stephanie, I wavered again. We lost her in May and I hardly went to church again for almost a year. I stopped tithing, because I was trying to deal with life. It took several years for me to regain my spirit and be on fire again. I went to a Bible study that one of my friends had at his home and we discussed dealing with money based on biblical principles. I grieved that I had stopped tithing. I let life get in the way again.

I grieved more because I never knew about a relationship with Jesus and that I had lived what I believed to be a Christian life without it.

Another lesson Pastor Chuck taught was about baptism. As Christians, we should invite Jesus into our hearts and profess our decision before man, as in going forward when the invitation to do so is made at the end of church services. We should be baptized the same way Jesus was baptized, by submersion.

I don't remember what the exact timeline was for these impactful lessons but the one I will never forget was when Pastor Chuck spoke about having a relationship with Jesus. I'd never heard it explained the way he explained it. The revelation I experienced that night made me grieve. Pastor Chuck explained everything that Jesus had done for us. He suffered and died on a cross because he loved us. And then Pastor Chuck made a statement that changed my life.

"And we don't deserve it, do we?" he asked.

I almost started crying and silently shook my head in agreement.

I gave my heart to Jesus that night. I wanted to be the Christian I should be in knowing Him.

A little later, closer to Easter, I decided I wanted to be baptized by submersion, the way Jesus was baptized. I had been baptized by sprinkling in the Methodist church. Carmon and I took a class when we were probably thirteen and fourteen. When we finished the class, we were baptized. I don't remember anything about the class. I don't remember the day we were sprinkled. I don't know I that consciously made the decision to be baptized. I feel it was made for me because of our age and that's what you do when you're that age and attend church. I just know that we did it.

I don't have anything against being baptized by sprinkling or attending a class to understand why you're being baptized, but for me, consciously making the decision to ask Jesus into my life and profess him publicly by being baptized the way He was—I'll remember that forever and I'll always know why I did it.

I woke up that Sunday morning and decided. Today was the day that I was going forward at the end of the service. I was going to profess Jesus before man and then be baptized.

And I did.

There were about fifteen of us who were baptized the Saturday night before Easter Sunday. I asked Jay to join me because he was my family. I also hoped that it would plant a seed for him and someday he would want to be baptized. He was carrying his Bible as he walked across the parking lot towards the main building that night. He also went to church with me the next day, Easter Sunday.

"I will walk with you if you want to go forward," I said.

During the invitation, I was supposed to be praying, head bowed, eyes closed. I was praying for Jay, but kept my eyes slightly open. I was watching Jay with my peripheral vision (I hope God had a sense of humor) to see if he started to make the move. I knew he would reach for my hand if he wanted to go forward, but he didn't.

Pastor Chuck asked us to invite someone to the service one Sunday.

"If you have someone you've been praying for, ask them to come with you. This could be the service that makes the difference," he said.

Jay rarely said no when I invited him to attend church with me and this Sunday was no different. During the service, members of the worship team acted out scenes of people who had problems and were talking with Christians who listened, tried to help them and hopefully lead them to Jesus. One scene was of a young man who was crying and told the person listening that his girlfriend died and he couldn't understand why God took her. It lasted too long for Jay and me.

When the service was over Jay practically ran out of the building, and so did I. Attending this service didn't give me the results I had hoped for. I wanted Jay to know Jesus like I did, but today would not be the day that it happened.

A few months later Jay relapsed again. When he stopped drinking, he ended up in a hospital. I sat with him through the night. He had removed the IV's, the heart monitor pads and the blood pressure cuff. I thought he was asleep from the medication he had been given. I sat next to the bed, my head resting on my arm on the bedrail. I had my other hand on Jay's thigh. I wanted him to know that he wasn't alone. I was trying in some way to help him. It was hard to see him suffer and not try to help.

The blood pressure machine kept beeping because he had taken the cuff off. He was sleeping but I wasn't getting any rest so to keep the machine quiet, I put the blood pressure cuff around my leg. It worked at first, but I woke up every time the machine tried to take my blood pressure.

Jay turned in the bed with his back to me and I pulled my hand away from his side.

"You can put your hand back on my leg," he said.

He had been resting, not sleeping. He was comforted by my being there.

Not long after that hospital visit, I paid for Jay to move back to Virginia, but he continued to struggle. He moved out of state to live with a sober friend who he met at Betty Ford. It was exciting to know he would be around someone he had been through therapy with. It gave me hope that this would be the thing that made the difference, but he was only there a few weeks when he moved back to Virginia.

I helped support him until one day when he called to ask for money. I told him no. In the past, I always hoped that the next move, the next job, the driver's license, the car, would be the thing to motivate him to stop drinking, but nothing did. I finally reached the point and accepted the fact that helping him was hurting him and if I continued, nothing would ever change. Something needed to change for him to be able to control his disease and live a normal life. I didn't want to see him suffer through hitting bottom to get better. But at this point, that seemed like the last resort. I regret that it took so long for me to realize it.

I had to stop helping him, enabling him, and force him to fend for himself. After a few days and another request for money, Jay knew that this time I meant it.

For me to help him again, he had to go to Teen Challenge, a treatment center that originally only treated teenagers but now helped all men and women. He finally relented and went against his will. He spent a short-term rehab there and left after four months of a one-year program. Again, he was completely sober. I felt he was even better this time because of the Christian influence at Teen Challenge.

Unfortunately, it didn't last and Jay relapsed once again.

CHAPTER 15

Where's Stephanie's Movie?

———

AFTER DREW PLANTEN'S DEATH THE news was full of information about the murder, his arrest, and suicide. Information that had been withheld awaiting a trial exploded across the news. I learned that he and his brother had been abused by their father when they were children. Their mother removed them from the home and moved away from the father.

And now, there were television shows about Planten and the crime. The first one was televised in 2009. Carmon let me know the day and time. I sat and watched as Stephanie's murder was exploited. Drew Planten was famous now. I kept the TV remote in my hand just in case something came on that I couldn't watch. Thankfully, I was able to turn it off quickly when they started reenacting the crime. I waited a minute, turned it back on, but quickly turned it off again. I had to do this several times before the show ended, and when it did I was thankful to see the real life Raleigh DA speak about Stephanie.

From the time of the murder until the end of this show, I worried that people would think Stephanie lived a life that would invite this crime. Maybe those feelings weren't warranted but that's how I felt. The DA said she had never met Stephanie personally but, through the investigation felt as though she had gotten to know Stephanie and her family, and could say with certainty that Stephanie did not deserve this. She said other nice things I don't remember, but for me, the show ended there. I turned the TV off; I wanted it to end with those comments about Stephanie and not the murderer.

Every now and then someone will come in my office, approach my desk in a quiet manner, and say, "I saw the show about Stephanie last night." It's almost always someone who met Stephanie when she lived and worked with me that summer between her junior and senior years at college. They could relate to what happened because they knew her. There have been other television shows about the murder, and even thirteen years later someone will tell me they've seen a rerun.

A friend in Ohio told me she and her husband were getting ready for bed when they turned their television on and saw me on the screen. It was a show about the murder, which surprised me because I hadn't been specifically interviewed for a TV show. I have not watched any of the reruns of the first show and am not interested in seeing any of the others. As recently as during my writing of this book, I have been contacted by another production company seeking comments on the murder from my viewpoint. I have not responded.

My question is, *Where is Stephanie's movie?*

Not a movie about the murder, Drew Planten, or the Raleigh police. But where is the movie about a young girl who had a beautiful smile and a sweet spirit, who was voted "Best Personality" by her senior class, who had graduated college and was just starting her career, who had moved to Raleigh where plans were being made for a future with her soon-to-be fiancé? Where's the movie about that girl?

When Stephanie was growing up, she could have decided not to be a good girl, but she didn't. She always wanted to do the right thing and worried if she thought she hadn't.

When she called that day to tell me that she'd been voted "Best Personality" by her high school senior class, I congratulated her but was surprised because she was so quiet most of the time. I guess when she was around her friends she blossomed. Her friends always remembered Stephanie. For several years in the fall, they held a fundraiser for the Memorial Scholarship Fund. At Christmas they visited Carmon, one time bringing a jar of memories of Stephanie they had written on pieces of paper. Another time Carmon and Jennifer went by the cemetery, and a few of her sorority sisters were sitting at her grave, crying.

One year on Stephanie's birthday, one of her friends posted on Facebook, "Happy Birthday in Heaven, Sweet Girl!"

Someone else commented on the post, "Growing up, I wasn't a wealthy kid with lots of nice things. I had enough. Stephanie saw one day in sixth grade that I didn't have a pen to write with, just an old pencil that had no eraser. She gave me this pretty pink pen that wrote so nicely! I always remembered her for that. She was always very kind to me. She was beautiful inside as well as out!"

Stephanie touched many lives during her twenty-three years of life. She touched even more in death.

My friend Rita Brinner did research for me and found a statement the assistant district attorney made during another television show, "Forencis Files – Calculated Coincidence."

Referring to a picture of Stephanie wearing a big purple felt hat with a red band, tacked on her wall above her desk in the courthouse, Susan Spurlin, Assistant District Attorney, said: "Every day when I walk into my office, I see Stephanie's picture. It is a picture that was taken of her smiling, of her having fun with her friends, having no idea that she would be dying at the hands of someone I believe was truly evil."

"I was disappointed that we weren't able to have a trial; that we weren't able to sit in the courtroom and hear a jury come back and say "You're guilty of the first degree murder of Stephanie Bennett and you have forfeited your right to live as a result of this crime."

From her book "Evil Next Door: The Untold Story of a Killer Undone by DNA" reporter Amanda Lamb writes that Spurlin kept the picture as a symbol of Stephanie's murder case and of all the murder cases she has prosecuted before and after Stephanie. "It reminds you that there are no guarantees for anyone tomorrow. There are no guarantees in this world for any of us."[iii]

The movie about Stephanie's life would end the way all movies based on a true story end. There would be several pictures of her and the last one would be a clip from a home video. When she realized she was being videoed, she turned around and smiled. The audience would see her smile, the radiance of her sweet spirit, and then they would cry.

Some TV shows and movies tell how the family of someone who wrecked and unintentionally killed another person forgave the person who caused the death, and sometimes I've heard how they either took them into their home or visited them in prison and then led them to Christ.

Before the arrest, I remember being in conversations about the person who murdered Stephanie and admitted I would kill him if I knew who it was and had the opportunity. I was angry; I was serious. Forgiveness was not part of the conversation. I never expected to hear myself saying that, but I had never expected to be in this situation.

After the arrest, I saw Drew Planten's slumped and lethargic position when he was wheeled into the courtroom, but I still had no sympathy for him. I felt bad for the little boy who suffered abuse at the hands of his father, the boy who should have been protected by his father. I almost felt that I could forgive that little boy.

But I could not forgive the man who made the decision to take the life of my niece, a young innocent girl, the man who knew the difference between right and wrong, the man who had taken two lives and was planning to take more, the man who premediated and intentionally raped and murdered my niece. I could not forgive this evil man. I *would not* forgive evil.

If forgiveness was in order, then it would have to come from God. It would be His decision.

CHAPTER 16

The Ministry Quilt

———

ONE OF MY EMPLOYEES, TINA, approached me one day and asked if I attended Crossroads Church. I told her about the two services I went to each Sunday and invited her to join me at whichever one she felt comfortable with. We met for the Sunday evening service the next weekend. I still sat in my usual seat far to the right, up eighteen steps in the seat on the aisle. When the service was over, we stayed seated and talked until we were about the only two people left in the building. I guess we both just needed to talk. She talked about the things that were currently going on in her life, and I shared about losing Stephanie, the murder, and how it was affecting my family and me. Tina met Jay when he worked with me. When she asked about him, I explained that he had moved back to Virginia and was struggling with alcoholism and depression. It felt good to finally share some of these things with someone who listened.

Tina continued to attend church with me, and one day at the end of the service when Pastor Chuck gave the invitation, I told her if she wanted to go forward I would go with her. She didn't go that day but did a few weeks later. On her own she stepped out, went forward, and was baptized that year at Christmas. Now whenever I'm asked if I've led anyone to Christ, I feel I can say yes.

Tina was ready to get involved. She wanted to attend a membership meeting and asked if I would go with her. This would be the first thing I did in five years besides attend the Sunday services. During my lifetime of attending church, I had played the piano or organ in church and had held several other ministry chair positions, but I'd been a recluse at this church. I felt it was time for me to be courageous and attend the meeting.

We learned about the different ministries and possible ways of serving. Tina selected the disabilities ministry. I, on the other hand, was more reserved and checked the box for the greeter ministry. I felt pretty safe with this. After all, I was only checking a box and probably wouldn't even be called to serve. If I was asked to serve, I thought I could say good morning to people. I wouldn't have to talk to them, and they didn't need to know my life's story.

Our next meeting was a ministries meeting for people who had volunteered to serve. Mark and Cheryl Peabody were in charge of the greeters ministry. They explained what greeting was about, what was expected, and where I would greet. I ended up greeting by myself, which was perfect for me, at the corner of the building next to a pillar. That pillar became my friend because I could hide behind it or lean on it. I didn't have to talk to it and, even if I did, it wouldn't talk back.

Services each Sunday morning were at nine and eleven. I greeted for the eleven o'clock service. So now instead of leaving the nine o'clock service through the side door and making a beeline to my car at the upper parking lot, I stood by my pillar and greeted people as they came up from the lower parking lot. At some point, I started parking in the lower lot so I could make another beeline to my car and leave once my greeting responsibilities were complete.

I learned from greeting people that not everyone wants to be greeted. How well I could relate to them! If people didn't make eye contact or respond to "Good Morning," I left them alone. I had no idea what was going on in their lives, and they didn't know that greeting them was a huge step for me.

The tool I used to approach someone I hardly knew but felt comfortable in approaching, came to me by accident. I was going to Virginia and wanted a small light-weight Bible that I could carry in my purse. I went to a Christian book store to find it and stopped at the current best seller shelves. It was there that I found my unexpected tool.

I picked the number two best seller at the time, *The Shack* "Where Tragedy Confronts Eternity" by William P. Young. I was on my flight from Orange County to Atlanta when I started reading it, and was surprised to find that it was about a little girl who was murdered by a serial killer and her father's relationship and interaction with God, Jesus, and the Holy Spirit on his journey to peace and forgiveness. I read part of it and had to put it down because I cried. A few minutes later I picked it up again, cried again, and stopped reading. I kept going through this cycle until I finished the book. It was hard for me to read but I had to finish it. I could relate to this book in a way that most people couldn't. In some ways I felt like I was reading my story.

I bought many more copies and gave them to friends I worked with and people at church I didn't yet know. In a way I was trying to open the door to communicate with them and let them know that I also had a story. Everyone thanked me for the book, but it didn't work. No one ever talked to me about the book after having read it.

I met many people from greeting every Sunday. I grew confident that I could connect with people and not live such an isolated life.

One Sunday I passed Mark and Cheryl on my way to the parking lot and they asked to let them know if I had any prayer requests.

I kept walking but when I burst into tears, I turned around, walked back to where they were, and asked them to pray for Jay. I explained that my nephew was an alcoholic and had moved back to Virginia but was having a rough time. They prayed for Jay right then.

I'm not exactly sure when they invited me to start sitting with them in church, but I left the safety of my aisle seat on the right side of the church and exchanged it for a seat beside Cheryl in what was probably the same exact row on the opposite side of the church. We became friends, and I started attending the Bible study at their home.

I eventually started greeting with Mark and Cheryl at what we refer to as "the rock," a large flat artificial rock about one foot high, in front of the church where people approached us from two parking lots. It's a high traffic greeting spot. Because people thought we looked alike, they assumed Cheryl and I were sisters. If Mark and Cheryl missed a Sunday, people asked where my sister was. She and I would explain that we were sisters in Christ but not earthly related.

Her father was also an alcoholic, and she had only had contact with him once since she was a child. She told me how, as an adult, she searched for him, found where he lived, and went to see him. She knocked on the door and introduced herself as his daughter. He told her he was just leaving but would be back soon. She waited, but he never returned, and she never saw him again.

Cheryl loves to sew and makes what I call ministry quilts. One ministry quilt was for a woman who had cancer. She personalized the quilt by printing a picture of the woman's family onto a piece of fabric and stitching it on the back of the quilt in one of the corners. She made a quilt and gave it anonymously to a local soldier who lost his leg. She had a passion for this ministry, using her ability to bless other people, and she wanted to make a quilt for Jay.

Cheryl didn't just make a quilt and hand it to me. She considered every step and every part of the quilt-making process important. First, we needed to decide on what color. Jay was a huge Carolina basketball fan and the Carolina blue was his favorite color, so that's the color I selected. Then we made trips to a few quilt shops to find blues, picking out several different shades and patterns.

The plan was for each block to have a white square in the center on which I would write a Bible verse. The white square would be bordered by eight points of the blue patterned fabric, forming a star, and then the star would be filled in with white fabric to complete the quilt square.

One Sunday morning as we sat in church, Cheryl handed me the white squares and a fabric pen along with a list of Bible verses she had used on another quilt. My job was to decide on the Bible verses I wanted to use and write them on the squares. These are the verses I chose.

* And do not go on presenting the members of your body to sin as instruments of unrighteousness; but present yourself to God as those alive from the dead, and your members as instruments of righteousness to God. *Romans 6:13*
* Therefore if anyone is in Christ, he is a new creature; the old things passed away; behold, new things have come. *2 Corinthians 5:17*
* For everyone who seeks finds, and to him who knocks it will be opened. *Matthew 7:8*
* All scripture is inspired by God and profitable for teaching, for reproof, for correction, for training in righteousness. *2 Timothy 3:16*

- For I know the plans I have for you, declares the Lord, plans for welfare and not for calamity, to give you a future and a hope. *Jeremiah 29:11*
- You scrutinize my path and my lying down. And are intimately acquainted with all my ways. *Psalms 139:3*
- The Lord is good to all, and His mercies are over all His works. *Psalms 145:9*
- And that from childhood you have known the sacred writings which are able to give you the wisdom that leads to salvation through faith which is in Christ Jesus. *2 Timothy 3:15*
- For the Lord will be your confidence and will keep your foot from being caught. *Proverbs 3:26*
- Casting all your anxiety on Him, because He cares for you. *1 Peter 5:7*
- Now faith is the assurance of things hoped for, the conviction of things not seen. *Hebrews 11:1*
- Create in me a clean heart, O God, and renew a steadfast spirit within me. *Psalms 51:10*
- But God demonstrates His own love toward us, in that while we were yet sinners, Christ died for us. *Romans 5:8*
- And I will be a father to you, and you shall be sons and daughters to Me, says the Lord Almighty. *2 Corinthians 6:18*
- But the fruit of the spirit is love, joy, peace, patience, kindness, goodness, faithfulness. *Galatians 5:22–23*
- The Lord is gracious and merciful; slow to anger and great in loving kindness, gentleness, self-control, against such things there is no law. *Psalm145:8*
- Come to Me, all who are weary and heavy-laden and I will give you rest. *Matthew 11:28*

- I can do all things through Him who strengthens Me. *Philippians 4:13*
- But the very hairs of your head are all numbered. *Matthew 10:30*
- For God so loved the world, that He gave His only begotten son. That whoever believes in him should not perish but have ever-lasting life. *John 3:16*

When Jay was a little boy, maybe four or five years old, I moved to California but was able to come home frequently because I traveled with my work. Every time I came home I brought him a T-shirt from where I'd been. I had a picture of me sitting on my mother's couch, holding Jay in my lap with my arms around him. We both had on T-shirts from Palm Springs. Cheryl asked for a picture to put in a corner of the back of the quilt, so I selected that one.

When I played the piano at Redwood Methodist Church, young Jay would sit with me on the front pew and sometimes on the piano bench while I played. One Sunday as we sat on the front pew, Jay had a Bible in his lap and asked me to give him a verse to find. I said *John 3:16*. He found it, looked at me to show me he had found it, and then asked for another one. Before I could say anything, the minister repeated the verse for the congregation as part of his sermon. Jay looked up at me with those little boy eyes and the look on his face told me he thought we had just experienced a miracle. That's the verse I chose to accompany the picture. I also asked her to include, "Always Remember That You're Loved."

She printed the picture on the left side of a piece of white fabric, the verse on the right side, and the words "Always Remember That You're Loved" a few spaces under the verse. She stitched a blue heart under the writing. We made another shopping trip for the quilt batting and selected one that would be the warmest for cold weather.

Jay was living in Virginia again but was out of state that year at Christmas. He was still struggling with alcoholism and depression. I sent the quilt to him as his present along with a letter telling him about Cheryl, how and why this quilt was made.

If I couldn't be with him and he couldn't be with our family, he would have this quilt to remind him that he was loved. When he saw the picture, the Bible verse, and the writing on the piece in the corner, I wanted him to know that Jesus would always love him and I would always love him, unconditionally. I was comforted by the fact that when he was using the quilt, he would be either covered with or wrapped in God's love.

CHAPTER 17

My 911 Call to God

WHILE ATTENDING CROSSROADS CHURCH, I learned that I should read my Bible daily and spend quiet time with God. I spent my quiet time with God after dinner every night sitting at my breakfast bar. Pastor Chuck encouraged us to read and then try to decide what God was telling us from the verses we read. What could we take from our reading and apply to our lives? Two of the times when I did this, I had immediate answers from God.

The first, I had finished reading my Bible and wondered what could I learn from this, what was God telling me? I was surprised when I instantly heard the Holy Spirit say, "Jesus is coming." I was stunned. I didn't hear it with my ears; I heard it inside my head. Nothing I read in those verses would have indicated that Jesus was coming, but the Holy Spirit wanted to tell me that He was.

The second time had to do with the homeless man we see at my work sometimes.

I was at lunch with my coworkers when the waitress asked if we wanted a to-go box for the food left on our plates. She suggested we take one and leave it at a trashcan in hopes a homeless person would find it. She shared that her brother was homeless by choice. He had a condition and refused to take his medication or live in the offered space at her home. She often suggests to customers that they leave their leftovers for the homeless. Hopefully, someone else was doing the same and her brother would be fed.

We often saw a homeless man digging through the trash at our office, so we took our leftovers to go. Not only did we take the leftovers from our meal, but the waitress also added rice, beans, tortillas, chips, salsa, and a package of plastic utensils with a napkin. This became our regular habit. We started looking for him and on most days found him in his usual spot under the freeway and were able to hand him his lunch.

This homeless man has never asked for money. He had good days and bad days. On the bad days he is in his own world, screaming, shouting, and waving his arms. We looked forward to giving him his meal every day.

People typically want to contribute when they know we're feeding the homeless. The waitress at another restaurant, after she took our to-go order for "a homeless man," came out of the kitchen with our order and said that everyone in the kitchen was impressed with what we were doing. Not only did we get the burrito but a bag full of chips, salsa, beans, plastic utensils, and napkins—probably enough food to feed a family of four.

Everyone at work called him "Kaye's homeless man" because I'm the one who started leaving food for him. Whenever we had a lunch at work, a barbeque or a Thanksgiving meal, I fixed a plate and took it to the trashcan in hopes he would get it and have a good meal that day.

One night I sat in my usual spot, reading my Bible and journaling. I thought about the homeless man. *He has to have a name. I wonder what it is?*

As soon as I had the thought, I heard the name "Anthony" inside my head. I was surprised but knew this was the Holy Spirit answering my question. A couple days later as we were leaving for lunch, our coworker Dave told us he saw our homeless man that morning when he came to work. He talked to him and asked what his name was. He said it was Anthony! I didn't share my story with them; I just smiled.

Another time I was reading in the book of Mark. I hadn't prayed and asked God to show me what this story meant, but he revealed it to me regardless. I read the story about the ruler whose daughter died. This man had faith that Jesus could just lay His hand on her and bring her back to life.

After He put them all out, He took the child's father and mother and the disciples who were with him, and went in where the child was. He took her by the hand and said to her, "Talitha koum!" (which means, "Little girl, I say to you, get up!). Immediately the girl stood up and walked around (she was twelve years old). At this they were completely astonished. He gave strict orders not to let anyone know about this, and told them to give her something to eat. *Mark 5: 21-43*

Tears came to my eyes when I read that he told her parents to give her something to eat. His love for her at that moment seemed larger than life to me. It was overwhelming. After what to me was such a huge miracle, he knew the young girl needed food and gave those simple instructions to her parents.

There had been other times when God communicated with me and I felt his presence. Once, while I was driving, he gave me a vision of something dark hitting the windshield. About thirty seconds later something the size of a pine cone or avocado fell out of a tree and hit the windshield right in front of my face.

"That was weird, but God if that was You, thanks for the heads-up."

He interacted with me at times when I didn't ask for it and least expected it. But now, I needed answers to prayers. I needed to hear from Him. I needed His help.

I was intentionally and constantly praying for Jay. I prayed for whatever his immediate need was, to get the job he wanted, to pass the bar exam. I thought that what I prayed for would be the one thing to get him on the right track and motivate him away from alcohol.

I wrote notes to Jay in my journal in the event that if he ever read them after I was gone, he would know that I prayed for him. It seemed I was always praying for the wrong things because he was still having problems—my prayers weren't working.

I prayed for God to reveal Himself to Jay so he would know and believe that God could and would help him. I even tried to convince God that Jay could do so much for Him, with his looks (Jay was voted "Best Looking" in his senior year of high school) and personality. People were drawn to Jay. He could be used to bring people to Jesus; of course, God already knew that.

One night during my quiet time, I read *Mark 9:29*: "And he said unto them, 'This kind can come forth by nothing, but by prayer and fasting.'" (KJV). I call this the 911 verse. Nine is the chapter number and the two numbers in the verse, two and nine, add to eleven.

When I read the verse, I thought, *This is the answer; this is what I can do, I can fast.* I was excited; there was still something I could do and it was biblical. Fasting was my 911 call to God. The next day at work I shared this with one of my employees, a friend Greg, who was a Christian and had also baptized me.

"I will fast with you," he said. He wanted to fast for his daughter.

Later that day another employee, also named Greg, came into my office, and I shared that Greg and I were going to fast. He wanted to join us and fast for his son.

Jantezen Franklin writes in his book *Fasting*, "In the Beatitudes, specifically in Matthew 6, Jesus provided the pattern by which each of us is to live as a child of God. That pattern addressed three specific duties of a Christian: giving, praying, and fasting. Jesus said, '*When* you give…' and '*When* you pray…' and '*When* you fast.' " He made it clear that fasting, like giving and praying, was a normal part of Christian life. As much attention should be given to fasting as is given to giving and to praying.

Solomon, when writing the books of wisdom for Israel, made the point that a cord, or rope, braided with three stands is not easily broken *Eccles. 4:12*. Likewise, when giving, praying, and fasting are practiced together in the life of a believer, it creates a type of threefold cord that is not easily broken. In fact, as I'll show you in a moment, Jesus took it even further by saying, "Nothing will be impossible" *Matt. 17:20.*"[iv]

I shared this with the two Gregs who were fasting with me and told them we also were a threefold cord that would not quickly be broken. Because as Christians we were asked to tithe, give our firsts back to God, we decided to fast on Monday, the first day of the week.

Matthew 6:16 says, "Whenever you fast, do not put on a gloomy face as the hypocrites do, for they neglect their appearance so that they will be noticed by men when they are fasting. Truly I say to you, they have their reward in full." I was anxious for my reward, which was Jay being cured and healthy.

The three of us began our fast. We fasted every Monday for over a year, eating nothing and only drinking water or tea. During our fast, I expected a miracle and looked forward to it, but it never came. Gradually each Greg broke their fast, and finally I gave in and ended mine.

Maybe the answer was no. There would be no reward.

I couldn't understand why God gave me a nephew, someone in my life whom I loved so much, who meant so much to me, and not allow him to have a life free of alcoholism. Worse, I had no assurance that he would be in heaven with me and with our family.

The only thing that mattered to me now was Jay's salvation. I had to accept the fact that alcoholism was winning or had already won. I didn't understand why fasting hadn't helped, but now my prayers were for his health, safety, and salvation.

Now I truly had to let go and let God. I had to trust that God was in control and He would take care of Jay.

CHAPTER 18
A Feeling of Dread

In 2008 I was in the airport after Christmas waiting for my return flight to California. My flight was delayed because of weather, then cancelled and rescheduled for the next day. Carmon came back to the airport and picked me up. I was at my mom's, sitting at the bar between the kitchen and dining room, on the phone with Jay. I told him about my cancelled flight and we were laughing about something.

My mom was in the entry room where her computer cabinet is. She was playing solitaire. I saw something out of the corner or my eye and glanced over to see that she was on the floor. I called to her but she didn't respond.

"Jay, I have to go; I've got to help Mom," I said with a sense of urgency.

I helped her get back in the chair, but she was incoherent. Thankfully there was a telephone in her computer cabinet and I called 911. Then I called Carmon, told him what happened and that I needed him to come to Mom's right away. He called me back in a couple of minutes and asked me what was wrong with her.

"I've called 911. I need you to come over here."

Carmon followed the ambulance from the highway. The first responders carried her outside and put her on a gurney. When they took her into the cold air, she came to. Carmon drove as we followed the ambulance to the hospital.

"I think I may have scared Jay," I said.

Carmon said he would call him when we got to the hospital.

My mom received fluids in the emergency room and was released. The doctor explained to her that she needed to stay hydrated. This was the beginning of my mom's health problems. After that episode, I started calling her twice a day, every day, to make sure she was okay.

Six month later, in May, my mom was having more problems. Jennifer took her to the doctor and she was sent to the hospital for an x-ray. The doctor wanted her to check into the hospital for gall bladder surgery but she refused because I wasn't there. I took a red-eye flight out of Los Angeles and arrived in Virginia on Saturday morning May 9. Carmon picked me up at the airport. We went to my mom's, picked her up and went to the hospital. Her surgery was Monday and she had to stay in the hospital for a couple of extra days because of dehydration.

This just happened to be the same week of Dee's wedding. My mom was released on Wednesday and we went to the wedding on Saturday. Everyone was surprised when they saw my eighty-three-year-old mother and how good she looked after just having had surgery. She looked better than I did; I was exhausted. My original flight was scheduled for Wednesday of that week and I had planned to shop for something to wear to Dee's wedding, but had flown to Virginia instead. I wore whatever it was I threw in my suitcase.

Stephanie and Dee had always planned to be each other's maid of honor and on May 16, 2009, the day of her wedding, Dee kept her promise. She placed a round table, the height of a tall nightstand, where the maid of honor would stand, next to the bride. The table was covered with a white cloth that touched the ground. The last bridesmaid came down the aisle carrying two bouquets. She placed one of them on the table, symbolizing that Stephanie was Dee's maid of honor. Dee also honored Carmon by asking him to walk her down the aisle, along with her brother, to give her away.

Dee's wedding weekend had been cloudy and stormy. It poured the night of the rehearsal. Since the wedding was outside, we were hopeful the wedding day would be clear. The day had been cloudy with rain at times, but when the ceremony was about to start, a ray of sunshine broke through the clouds and placed itself right on the event and the sky cleared.

We smiled and thought, "Hey, Stephanie!"

In July, my boss invited a few of us to Colorado to go river rafting. I was excited to go somewhere other than Virginia, and while I had never been rafting, I have always enjoyed being on the water.

We got up early to drive to the river, got out of the vehicles and walked to the river's edge. The three rafts were moored next to the bank. They each had a seat in the center for the guide where the oars were, one in the front of the raft and another seat in the back. One of the rafts had a back seat duck taped to the raft.

"I'm not sitting in that seat," I said.

As soon as I said it, my friend Greg and I were told that was our raft and the duck taped seat was mine. They were doing me a favor by giving me this seat because the person in the front seat usually gets wet from splashing water.

The other people in our group boarded their rafts and started down the river. I noticed that their guides were young and buff. Our guide wasn't. As we began our trip down the river, our guide told us that he'd had a midnight rafting trip the night before with some of his friends. Not only was he not young and buff, he was tired.

Our ride down the river that morning was uneventful. Greg caught all the fish because he was sitting in the front. I wasn't really interested in fishing; I couldn't cast the line like you're supposed to anyway. I just wanted to enjoy the scenery and the experience.

We stopped for lunch, ate sandwiches, and then resumed our trip.

This time I sat in the front of the raft, so I could maybe catch a fish. Not long after we started down the river, a storm approached. The wind was so strong my hat went flying. We all got wet from the rain, and being in the front seat, I also got splashed. We stopped, took another break and when it was over, I asked to have my duck taped seat back.

We continued down the river and our ride was almost over. The other two rafts were in front of us, one was out of sight around a bend, but the other one was close to us. We watched as it went head-on through the last of the whitewater for the day. Our raft approached the whitewater and instead of hitting it head-on like we should have, our guide made a mistake. The raft turned sideways, rolled over and dumped us into the cold river. In the instant of a heartbeat, I was under water, deep under water. My prescription sunglasses lifted from my face.

When I surfaced, I couldn't get my breath. I was choking. In the next instant I went under again. When I surfaced this time, I still couldn't breathe. If I went under again, I wouldn't make it; this could be it for me. I had to get air somehow. Finally, I was able to get a bit of air, then another bit. I continued to gasp and cough. The side of the upside-down raft was in my face and all I could see was blue rubber. I kept trying to grab hold of something but all I got was wet rubber. There was nothing to hang onto. I heard Greg calling my name.

"Kaye, are you alright?" he asked.

He had worked his way around to the end of the raft and I saw his face was covered with blood.

This is bad, I thought.

I kicked my feet, trying to push the raft in the direction of the bank. It seemed to be working. What I didn't know was that Greg was on the other side trying to pull it toward the bank.

Our guide yelled to his friend in the raft in front of us. They made their way over to the bank and were starting to climb over large rocks to get to us. Our guide also yelled and asked if we held onto his equipment.

"Are you kidding me?" I didn't say it out loud, but really? Here I am half-drowned and he wanted to know if I had his fishing gear in my hand?

We finally made it over to the shore and I was hugging a rock for dear life. My friend and co-worker Dave came to where we were and reached out a hand to me.

"Take my hand and I'll help you out of the water," he said.

"I can't, I don't have the strength," I said.

Dave literally grabbed my lifejacket and pulled me up out of the water onto another rock. I couldn't move. I sat there shivering and stunned (maybe more like shocked) at what I'd just experienced. Greg was already out of the water, his face cleaned of the blood, and our guide had made his way back to where we were. The men flipped the raft over.

"Do you want to climb the bank to the highway and be picked up there or would you rather ride the raft and be picked up downstream?" Dave's guide asked.

"How far is it to the end?" I asked.

"It's just around the next bend."

He pointed and showed me. I looked and saw that the water was calm. There was no way I could climb to the highway, so I agreed to ride the raft.

My rafting trip didn't turn out like I had expected. I emailed Carmon and Jay about what happened, asked them to not tell my mom, and told them I was okay.

Two minutes after I sent the email, Jay called me.

"What do you mean by putting yourself in harm's way?" he asked.

"Our family has been through enough. Are you sure you are okay? Don't ever do anything like that again."

I would have felt the same way Jay did, if it had been him. He was right.

Over the next couple of years, I visited Virginia often. I was working in Ohio as a consultant with another company that my boss owned, and at the end of those work weeks, I went to Virginia, spent the weekend, and flew back to California on Sunday. My mom liked that I came home often for short visits; I liked it, too, because I got to check on her.

In May of 2013, I planned a long weekend trip home. I was going to present the scholarship from Stephanie's Memorial Fund, but my mother was sick again and she wouldn't go to the emergency room until I got there. I took another red-eye flight out of Los Angeles. Carmon picked me up at the airport. When I walked in my mom's house, I saw her and asked Carmon to call 911. This time it was stomach ulcers and they did surgery the next day to enlarge the opening from her stomach to her small intestines. She was hospitalized for several days because she was dehydrated.

The award ceremony was in the high school auditorium on Wednesday night of that week. I had stayed in the hospital with my mom day and night and I was exhausted.

I had prepared to present the award, but wasn't sure if I was up to it. A friend of our family was on standby in case I wasn't able to do it.

Carmon stood with me on stage that night; he always stood with the person who presented the scholarship.

"Good evening and congratulations to the Class of 2013. My name is Kaye Bennett and I am here on behalf of the Stephanie Bennett Memorial Scholarship Fund. Stephanie Bennett was my niece. The day my brother took her to Roanoke College to move into the dorm, he called me and said that when he left her, she was crying. He asked me to call her and see if she was okay. I waited until the next afternoon before making the call and on my third attempt, she finally answered the phone.

'Stephanie, I've been trying to call you,' I said.

'I've been at a freshman orientation and am on my way to a social event that one of the sororities is having for the new students. Is it okay if I call you back tomorrow?' she said.

"I knew then that she was going to be okay. Stephanie blossomed in college. She entered college as a young girl and graduated four years later as a young woman.

"One of her friends later told us that she wouldn't have made it through college if it hadn't been for Stephanie's support and encouragement. That same friend wrote a poem about her that was read at a bench dedication at Roanoke College. *The best way to describe her is that she was the sweetest little thing, a breath of fresh air, the wind beneath our wings.*

"We celebrate Stephanie's life through this scholarship along with the continued spirit of support and encouragement. Please join me in honoring this year's recipient of the $7,500 Stephanie Bennett Memorial Scholarship, Miss Megan Vest."

I only faltered once, when I read the line from the poem. My voice cracked; I had a hard time getting those words out. The graduates laughed when I told them what Stephanie said the day I called her. Their laughter helped relieve my tension and Megan Vest was very appreciative, hugging and thanking me twice.

Whenever I was in Virginia, I always spent time with Jay. We went to movies, to dinner, or he would come to my mom's and visit. For most of his adult life, he called me two or three times a week and I could always count on him to call me on Sundays. After I finished greeting on Sunday and walked to my car, I checked my phone and saw that he had called.

"I just wanted to hear a friendly voice," Jay said almost every time I called him back.

We had always talked every day when I was in Virginia, but things had changed. There were times when I didn't get to see Jay. We made plans for me to visit him, see a movie or have dinner, but then he would cancel.

I went to Virginia on Labor Day Weekend 2014 for my mom's eighty-eighth birthday. I called Jay and he said yes, I could come see him. When I saw him, he had lost weight, but looked good. Jay always looked good; he was so handsome. He also looked young. Everyone always told me that I didn't look my age. At forty, Jay didn't look his age, either. He said he didn't feel good; he could have had a bug or something, but I expected it to be the end of a detox. I was always suspicious.

When I saw him that day, he gave me a birthday present, a Los Angeles Angels t-shirt and also a birthday gift for my mom. I visited with him for about twenty minutes. He walked me to the door and we hugged.

"I love you, Jay," I said.

"I love you, too!" he said, and then gave me a kiss on the cheek.

Two months later I planned another weekend trip, this time to New York.

I met Greg and Elsa Ellingson when they joined our home group at the Peabody's. They had three children, two girls and a boy, and had attended Crossroads for a few years. As we got to know each other, we realized that when we first attended we both sat on the same side for a few years, never speaking to anyone. They actually sat in front of me, a few rows closer to the floor.

Their daughter Kristen graduated from high school and was going to start interviewing for a part time job before she began college in the fall. I suggested to Elsa that she have Kristen come by my office and I would have her go through the interview process so she would feel a little more comfortable when she started interviewing. She came by and filled out the application. I interviewed her and was so impressed, I hired her myself. Kristen came into my office every day. We became friends, and I became her mentor.

The Ellingson family camped but had not traveled out of state a lot. I went to Virginia often, and Kristen imagined the places she would like to travel and added Virginia to her list. Another family in our home group, the Marshs, had a daughter, Sakkara, who recently moved to New York. I had always wanted to see a play in New York, so I suggested we add that to our wish list.

I received a travel voucher from Delta Airlines for a companion ticket where two could fly for the price of one. When I checked the flights from Los Angeles to New York, the price for a single ticket was reasonable.

"I think we need to make this happen. Let's plan a weekend and go to New York," I said to Kristen.

I heard myself invite her but couldn't actually believe that I had. A feeling of dread came over me like a shroud the instant I said it. Ever since Richard died on his way home after taking me to meet friends to go to the beach, I had a dread of traveling away from home, a dread that something would happen. When I traveled for work, the feeling of dread wasn't there. When I traveled for pleasure, the feeling was always there to some degree, and here it was again—really strong this time. I couldn't understand why it was so strong, and it was a little scary. It was only for a long weekend. It seemed so simple, so do-able. I kept telling myself I needed to fight this feeling. I could do this. I could get over this feeling when I travel. I could go to New York, have a good time, and everything would be okay.

Kristen texted me that night to tell me her parents said she could go. I honestly thought that if her parents said no, this feeling of dread would go away, and I would feel better. No trip, no feeling of dread.

Just like every other Sunday, I had a call from Jay the week before our trip.

"I sent you a card with a little gift in it. Did you get it?" He asked.

"No, I haven't," I said.

We talked for a little and then hung up. On Tuesday, he called and I told him I got the card. Jay was so sweet and thoughtful, but I could tell he was struggling. It always hurt to hear him like this.

On Thursday of that week, November 6, 2014, Kristen and I flew to New York. Kristen had never flown before but she enjoyed the flight. She was nervous but excited. Flying with her that day reminded me of the times I had traveled with Jay and Stephanie. It was cold and raining when we arrived. We took a car from the airport to our hotel in Times Square. After we checked in, I called my mother to let her know I had arrived and everything was okay.

Sakkara and Kristen met each other for the first time that night at dinner. Eating in New York was an adventure, but even with all the variety to choose from, we chose hamburgers and french fries at the restaurant Sakkara selected for us. It wasn't your ordinary hamburger and fries. Being in New York, they were special, so we took pictures. We were foodies, or at least we liked the presentation. I've always said, "Presentation is everything!"

Time zone change and jet lag had never agreed with me. When we got back to our hotel, we enjoyed the view of Times Square for a little while and then I got ready for bed. Kristen told me she would be in the bathroom talking to her boyfriend and parents and to let her know if she was too loud. I think I possibly heard her say two words before I fell asleep.

The next morning we slept in a little to stay on the same time as California, and I called my mother again. After that, Kristen and I began our adventure as tourists. We started in the hotel at a coffee shop and had a bagel with cream cheese and coffee, taking our time and enjoying watching other people. A bus tour was recommended, so we bought two tickets, and rode through the streets of New York. Kristen especially wanted to see the Statue of Liberty. She brought her new camera and was looking forward to taking pictures.

We rode the tour bus through the city, passing several well-known buildings and had a two-second window where we could see the Statue of Liberty. Kristen missed it. We got off the bus before the tour ended and walked a couple of blocks to see Rockefeller Center. A crane was lifting the tree that would be decorated for the Christmas season. It was interesting to see it being put in place. We went through a few shops and gradually made our way back to the hotel, passing Radio City Music Hall.

Ever since my mother started having health problems, I called her every morning and night to check in and make sure she was okay. When we arrived back at the hotel, I called one more time to tell her we would be going to dinner and the Broadway show "Wicked" and would not call again that day. I was making it through this feeling of dread.

Kristen and I went back to the same shop where we had break-fast and got some fruit and cheese for a snack so we wouldn't spoil our dinner. Sakkara selected another restaurant for us that evening, and we were to meet her at six. While we were resting and munching, we made plans to see another play on Saturday.

Our evening began with a subway ride to meet Sakkara. I downloaded the subway app for the New York subway system on my iPhone and thought I had the route all worked out. We went to the subway station, bought the tickets, and got on the subway. I'm not ashamed to say I was totally confused. We were on the subway at the worst time of day, Friday night at five thirty, when everyone was going home from work. We were sardines in a can; sardines that didn't speak to each other. Kristen and I were reviewing the route. All of a sudden it got confusing, and I couldn't figure out where we were. When I was in England, the subway had a map of the stations on the inside and I could see where I was all the time. This subway had nothing but wall-to-wall people.

As I tried to figure it out, someone told us where we should get off and which train to take from there. No one was talking to anyone else on this train, but they were listening. When the train stopped, we got off in the midst of people running everywhere. We tried to find a sign that would help us. Another person who had overheard us pointed to the train we were supposed to take. We went to the spot, but it just didn't make sense to us that we should go that way. Kristen and I decided we didn't want to take the subway, so we went up to the street to find a cab. What we found was hardly one person in sight in either direction, which was a little scary. A taxi came by within a couple of minutes, and we were able to take it to the restaurant. Thank You, Jesus.

When we arrived at the restaurant, Sakkara was already waiting. We had to tell her our subway story. We had a relaxing dinner, and again took pictures of our food. After dinner we decided we had time to walk the twenty blocks to the theatre instead of taking a cab. It seemed everyone in New York walked a lot. We walked the mile or so and still arrived at the theatre early.

Everything Kristen saw and experienced that day was exciting for her. The play was no exception, but for me, it could have been better. I'm sorry, New York, but I thought when I saw a play on Broadway it would be by far the best performance in the country. This one let me down. The person who played the lead role of Elphaba did not do the songs justice.

When the play was over, we were standing in front of the theatre, deciding whether to take a taxi or walk back to the hotel. I checked my phone and saw that Carmon had sent a text that read, "Call me, it's an emergency." When I saw it, I said out loud, "This can't be good." Carmon had never sent that kind of text, so I knew something was wrong and it was bad.

"I got your message," I said.

"Have you talked to anyone?" He asked.

"No, I just walked out of a theatre. Why?"

"Jay died."

When Carmon called to let me know that Stephanie died, I didn't even ask him what happened because I was in shock. I made sure that I didn't make that mistake this time, although I felt that I already knew the answer.

"What happened?" I said.

"His roommate came home from work and found him."

Jay had been detoxing and didn't survive it this time.

For one fleeting moment I thought, *He doesn't have to suffer with alcoholism anymore.* In the next moment, the reality of the news I'd just heard swept over me. I found myself in another state of shock and started crying. I always felt that I might get this call but was not prepared for it. Another phone call that changed my life! The loss of the last child in our family! How much could one family bear?

I realized that the feeling of dread was God's way of telling me something bad was going to happen, just like I felt the night Richard died. As I look back on this trip to New York, I feel it was orchestrated by God. I was in New York and able to get to Virginia quicker than if I'd been in California. Unfortunately, I had to leave Kristen in New York by herself for a few hours before she was able to board a flight back to California. She had never been alone like that in her life, but said she wasn't afraid. I hugged her when I left at four in the morning and assured her she would be all right.

I tried to convince myself of the same thing.

I will be all right.

CHAPTER 19

Jesus Decides

MY FLIGHT TO ROANOKE LEFT Newark, New Jersey at six thirty in the morning with a change of planes at Dulles International. When I arrived at the airport, an announcement was made asking people who could postpone their travel plans and take a later flight to approach the counter because the flight was oversold.

I could only imagine what I looked like. I had been awake and crying all night and was reliving the shock I had experienced several times before in my life. Unfortunately, I knew what was in front of me for the next few days and the next year. I had to say goodbye to my nephew, and endure another visitation, another funeral, another year of firsts, and another struggle to figure out what the new normal would be and to live it.

Because my reservation had been made only a few hours earlier, I felt that I might get bumped. When I went to the counter to explain that there had been a death in my family and if at all possible I needed to board this flight and get to Virginia as soon as I could, the girl behind the counter acknowledged me. I thought I might have looked a little scary. A few minutes later she motioned for me to come to the counter and when I did, she told me that I could board the plane. I was the first passenger to board, went to the rear of the airplane, and sat in the window seat in the last row on my left. Thankfully, the majority of the passengers did not see me.

I changed planes in Dulles without any problem, sat in a window seat in the rear of the plane and gazed out the window the entire flight. Sometimes I nodded off but waking instantly when I did. The pilot announced our final approach into the Roanoke airport, and through tears, I recognized familiar landscape as the plane descended. It was just after sunrise, morning had broken and the blue skies and white clouds had the promise of a new day. The trees cast long dark shadows on the green fields. My day wouldn't be filled with blue skies and white clouds. My day would be filled with long dark shadows.

My thoughts turned to some of the happy homecomings there had been over the years. The time when I brought the large stuffed animal "Butch the bulldog" to Jay when he was a little boy. The time when Jay and Stephanie were supposed to pick me up but weren't there when I arrived. They were parked at the airport listening to "(Everything I Do) I Do It for You", the song from the movie Robin Hood. The first time I came home after Stephanie and Dee spent the summer with me, they surprised me and picked me up at the airport. I thought about the many other times when Jay and Stephanie were there to greet me.

When the plane touched the runway, I snapped out of my reverie.

Jennifer, my sister-in-law, picked me up in Roanoke. Carmon had outpatient knee surgery the day Jay died but hadn't told his son about the surgery because Jay would have worried. Jennifer told me that when Carmon learned that his son died, he became physically ill.

When we arrived at their home, Carmon was sitting at the breakfast bar with his back to me, his knee elevated and crutches leaning against the bar. I walked up behind him and gave him an awkward hug around his shoulders. When I stepped around and saw his face, it was apparent that he was still fighting the nausea and sickness that accompanied it. He had eaten breakfast and was trying to keep it down.

Carmon had lost both of his children. Our family was getting smaller. There were three of us left. Richard, Stephanie, and Jay were all gone now.

At the same funeral home, the same chapel where Stephanie's visitation had been, we stood through another visitation. It lasted over four hours. Jay was cremated, so there was no funeral but a memorial service the next day. The chapel and adjoining rooms were overflowing.

Jay's friend Bradley gave the eulogy. "What do you say about a person you have known forever? Someone you have called a friend, roommate, teammate, and even a brother from another mother. What can you say about someone who was loved by so many that would do him justice? Jay was so smart, crazy smart, like never open a book and know the answers smart. His potential knew no limits. Jay was caring, loving, and loyal, all the things you look for in a friend. The girls loved him and the guys wanted to be him. It was impossible to meet him and not be drawn to his soul and presence. He was truly special."

Shane Nerenberg, who Jay lived with in California, spoke after Bradley and shared a conversation he had with Jay one day when they were riding the eight miles into town.

"Jay asked what I call the 'Why God,' questions," Shane said. "Why would a God of love allow this to happen to my sister? If God loves us so much, why didn't He stop this? Why would a God of love allow sickness and suffering? Why would a God of love allow us to suffer so much pain?"

'I don't have the answered to all of those questions,' I told him. 'I have asked some of the same questions at times in my life. The person who did this to Stephanie will be judged by the one true Judge, God Himself. You and I will be judged by God Himself and His judgement will be just and true. The good news is that the scriptures tell us that God is also love and that he is gracious and compassionate. In His wisdom, God provided a just pardon from the death sentence. A just, perfect man had to die in my place, in your place. That Man was Jesus. He paid the penalty and satisfied the judgment for you and me. If you believe that, in faith, you are pardoned and forgiven, NOTHING can separate you from the love of God.'"

"Jay turned away and looked out the window in silence. I could almost hear his legal mind processing what he had just heard. After a moment or two of silence Jay turned to me and said, 'I believe that makes more sense than anything else I have heard before.'"

The day after the memorial service, my mom and I were sitting across from each other at the small bar between the kitchen and dining room. We had finished dinner and were playing games on our iPads, mostly going through the motions, neither of us saying much, but periodically crying and grieving. I was distraught. Not only did I have to deal with the fact that Jay was gone and that we were facing another year of firsts without him, but more importantly I didn't know for sure if he was in heaven. I knew he hadn't been baptized and he told me once that he had issues with the resurrection. And, as far as I knew, he hadn't invited Jesus into his life.

I sat staring at my iPad, anxious. I had to know and finally got the courage to ask, afraid of the answer. I didn't say it out loud but silently asked Jesus, "Is Jay with You?" Within less than an instant, these thoughts were in my mind:

You fasted for two years. I brought the young girl back to life because of her father's faith and then told them to give her something to eat.

I was surprised and wondered why I was thinking about my fasting and Bible study. And then I realized that Jesus was answering my question! The thoughts quickly continued.

The Lord will fuss at him a little bit. The angels ministered to Jesus after He'd been in the desert and fasted for forty days. The Lord will fuss at him a little bit.

Then the words "in the arms of the angels fly away" and music from the song "Angel" repeated in my mind like a broken record.

I was so taken with this experience that I had to leave the room. Not only had Jesus answered my question but He also told me how my nephew left this world, in the arms of angels who were ministering to him. And then my thoughts turned to the class I attended when Pastor Barry was still at Crossroads. Our study that night was based on *John 14:6*: "Jesus said to him, 'I am the way, the truth, and the life; no one comes to the Father but through me.'" Pastor Barry challenged us to discuss this verse and determine its meaning. We basically determined that it meant Jesus decides who goes to the Father; Jesus decides who goes to heaven. And Jesus had decided.

Jesus answered me in an instant. He knew how important it was to me and that I needed to know. Jesus told me I fasted for two years. It was actually one year and two or three months, but He gave me credit for two years. I specifically remember how I felt when I read the story about Him bringing the little girl back to life, how much He loved her when after this miracle he instructed her parents to give her something to eat. It was another one of those larger than life moments. How could I have known then what it would mean to me now?

He also told me twice that God was going to fuss at Jay a little bit. Jay was a good person but didn't live a Christian life. I thought that applies to all of us, though; none of us were perfect and might experience God "fussing at us a little bit." Jay was detoxing the night he died. I knew firsthand how he suffered through it. Knowing the angels ministered to him as they carried him away was so comforting. I could only imagine what Jay experienced. He deserved to be ministered to because of all his suffering with his disease.

In the next few minutes after Jesus answered me, I was able to wrap my mind around what I just experienced. I realized that it wasn't my courage that caused me to ask Jesus if Jay was with Him. The Holy Spirit forced me to ask because Jesus was waiting to answer. When He answered, I was reeling in the moment. I thought of two things I had done in my life that I'm not proud of and realized that Jesus loved me anyway.

My eyes were opened and I knew the simplicity of His love. I was overwhelmed and humbled by it. I later realized that it not only was about how much Jesus loved me but also how much He loved Jay. My prayers had been answered. For all of those years when I prayed, Jesus had been listening and He acknowledged my fasting.

Although it had been less than two weeks since I returned to California, I went back to Virginia to spend Thanksgiving weekend with my family. While there, I was given the ministry quilt and letter (he had saved it) I had sent Jay. The newness of the quilt was gone and the Bible verses were faded a little from being washed.

I heard my first Christmas carol on my way to work the Monday morning after Thanksgiving. I listened to KSGN Christian radio, and starting on Thanksgiving Day they played nothing but Christmas music. I didn't know what a panic attack was until the music started playing. When I heard the music, the reality that Stephanie and Jay were both gone and would not be there for Christmas caused me to feel intense fear and I couldn't breathe. I quickly turned the radio off and tried to push those thoughts from my mind so I would relax and breathe.

The realization that I had just experienced a panic attack frightened me. I would have to try and block Christmas out of my mind to prevent other attacks. Thankfully it worked, for then.

I downloaded the songs "Amazing Grace" by Willie Nelson and "Hallelujah" by Jeff Buckley, two of the songs played at the memorial service. "Hallelujah" was one of Jay's favorite songs, and Willie Nelson one of his favorite artists. I also downloaded "Angel" by Sarah McLachlan, the "in the arms of the angels" song. I played these songs as I got ready for work and drove to and from work, instead of listening to Christmas carols.

Dee knew Christmas would be hard for us, so she brought her family to Rocky Mount. They came to my mother's for Christmas Eve dinner. Having two little boys running around enjoying Christmas helped, but it was still a struggle.

"Granny Bennett, can we please open the presents before you wash the dishes?" Dee's four-year-old Jake politely asked as we finished eating dinner.

How many times had we heard this over the years from Jay and Stephanie? Of course, Granny Bennett said yes. We went into the living room and, as had been our custom for so many years, the youngest child passed out the presents. Dee's boys were too little to read the names so we helped them. Watching them hand the presents to everyone and wade through the discarded wrapping paper on the floor, going from one person to another to see everyone's gifts, was surreal. That same living room had once included Richard, Jay, and Stephanie on similar Christmas Eves.

We went to Carmon's on Christmas Day. As Dee was showing the gifts her boys received from Santa, I glanced up to the fireplace mantel and saw pictures of Jay and Stephanie. It was a heart-wrenching moment.

When we lost Stephanie, I drank beer for four or five months. Now that we'd lost Jay, I drank again. This time it was beer, wine, or whatever I hoped would get me to a point where I would neither think nor feel. I drank a lot, too much really, every night. I was grieving, dealing with panic attacks, and trying to cope with the reality that there were no more children in our family. My father was gone, my mom was eighty-eight, and because Carmon was only slightly older than me, statistically I felt I would outlive him and end up alone with no family whatsoever. I became very depressed.

On Tuesday of the week Jay died, I received a card from him. The front read, "Go Outside and Set the World on Fire." On the inside he had written, "Hey Auntie! I sure do love you!" He sent a Los Angeles Angels baseball decal in the card. Jay was always so thoughtful.

Not only could I not go outside and set the world on fire, I was beginning to wonder if I'd ever feel normal again, or exactly what normal would mean now.

I kept the card he'd sent and a heartfelt note from one of his previous girlfriends in my open Bible as I sat and drank each night. His girlfriend had written, "I know Jay and I have not been close in many years, but I can say with certainty that he had an enormous, loving heart of gold." And I can say with certainty that she is right. I would miss him, his hello and goodbye hugs, his goodbye kiss on the cheek, his phone calls and the thoughtful things he would always say and do.

As Christians, we are not exempt from grief. We were not promised a life free of problems, trouble, or pain. We have no guarantee that bad things wouldn't happen to us or our loved ones. I knew Jay was in heaven. I knew he was carried there in the arms of angels who ministered to him. I knew he was with his sister, my brother, and my dad. I couldn't have asked for more. All that mattered was that Jay was in heaven. But I still had to go through the grieving process and learn to live without him in my life.

Finally, in April after Jay passed, I decided it was time to stop drinking and start trying to live my new normal, whatever that would be.

I've always felt that I had a sermon in me somewhere, but like Moses I have been "slow of speech and slow of tongue" *Exodus 4:10.* Some of my friends might not agree with me because I was quick to respond to their wisecracks and creative with my comebacks. But I have always been soft-spoken and have never been a public speaker. After Richard died I learned to not talk about my grief. People didn't want to hear about it because it was easier for them. After we lost Stephanie and I finally reached the point where I wanted to talk about it, I would tell people, "I have a story." I gave away copies of *The Shack* by William P. Young to people I knew and some I didn't. I was trying to open the door so I could tell them about "my story."

Previously when I told people I had a story, the story was about our family, about me, about what happened in our lives. Now we had also lost Jay, and I had another story about what happened to our family, what happened to me. But now it's different.

This time the story was about Jesus and the night He answered my question, "Is Jay with You?" At first I shared my story with only a few close friends. After a few months, when I felt I could talk about it without crying, I shared the story with my life group. I only told people who were Christians, those who would understand and know that it was real.

Now I was writing a book, which would surprise a lot of people. It's actually surprising me. When I told a previous employer about my project, he said, "You can't even write a letter." Well, it's true, I can't write a letter. My response to him was, "It's not a letter; it's a book."

Those times when I felt I had a sermon inside me that was trying to get out, or when I wanted to tell everyone about losing Richard, about Stephanie, her murder, and our survival of it, it wasn't a sermon. It was my story. But God wasn't through with me. I had to experience losing Jay so He could show me Jesus's love. God had been listening to my prayers and acknowledged my fasting, so I could experience Him in an intimate way.

My story had an ending now and was ready to be shared. It's about Jesus's love, how He loves all of us and answers our prayers. Even when we think He's not listening, He answers our prayers in His time.

And now, because of my life experiences, I had come full circle and understood the true meaning of the all the words in the hymn I played as a child. I understood life with no peace. I understood needless pain. I understood grief all too well. More importantly,

I understood and *knew* the true meaning of 'What a Friend We Have in Jesus.'

I knew I would experience more loss and grief in my lifetime, but because of His love, I now lived with a peace and joy that I'd never known before.

EPILOGUE
CALLING ALL ANGELS

In October of 2002, only five months after Stephanie died, Jay called to see if we could get tickets to an Angels game. It was the first postseason series and the Angels were playing the New York Yankees. Jay was a huge Yankee fan. All I cared about was spending time with him. At the time, it had only been five months since we'd lost Stephanie, and I took every opportunity to see him. My work had a suite at Angels stadium and great seats between home plate and first base. I asked my boss if there were any tickets left for the game. There were, and we got those seats.

Jay was amazed and excited that he was actually at a major league baseball postseason game, and I started to realize just how special this was. I was so happy for Jay that we were able to sit so close to the field.

"I can see my Yankees almost up close and personal." Jay said.

He came from San Diego, brought a friend, and we met another one of his friends at the game. That night, for the first time in several months, my thoughts were taken away from the reality of what was going on in our lives. I sat next to Jay and listened to the conversations he had with his friend. Watching him enjoy this was doing as much for me as attending the game was for him.

At one point, one of the Angels players hit a home run.

"He kissed that ball and sent it out of this ball park," Jay's friend said.

The Angels went on to win the game, beating the Yankees in the first round of postseason play. Jay was sad that the Yankees lost but intended to support the Angels going forward in the post-season.

The Angels beat the Minnesota Twins in the American League Division Series and were into game six of the World Series against the San Francisco Giants. Jay and I went to the game. He dressed like a true Angels fan. He wore an Angels jersey and had a rally monkey hanging around his neck.

At the World Series, every pitch was important, so we stood almost the entire time. We were in the seventh inning and the Angels were behind. It appeared that the San Francisco Giants would be celebrating a World Series win at Angels stadium. I remember standing next to Jay, thinking it had been a bad year for us already and now the Angels were probably not going to win. I wanted them to win so we would have something to celebrate, something to cheer about. I wanted us to have one more day of a reality-free life.

Scott Spiezio came to bat. He had a full count with two men on base and hit a three-run home run, putting the Angels in the game and changing the momentum of the entire series. The Angels went on to win game six. There would be no San Francisco Giants World Series celebration in Angels Stadium that night!

Then we were at game seven, same seats in the stadium, same jerseys, same rally monkeys, and again standing for every pitch. Troy Percival threw the last pitch, and the Angels won the game when Darin Erstad caught the fly ball in center field for the third out. That moment was so huge, it was hard to take it in. The crowd went wild! We literally felt the stadium shake when everyone jumped at the last out. Confetti and streamers shot out of the top of the stadium, and fireworks lit up the night sky. Jay nudged me and pointed to the freeway; the traffic was at a standstill. The Angels won the 2002 World Series and we were there to see it. It was an amazing experience and now a beloved memory.

I fell in love with baseball during the 2002 World Series when I was there with Jay. We had two complete days of not having to think about what had happened in our lives. Angels baseball took us to a place away from our reality. I was excited for the next season to start, and when it did, I got tickets and went to a few games with Jay. But sometimes I bought a single ticket and went by myself.

I tell everyone that Angels baseball saved my life.

Now, when I go to Angels games, the song "Calling All Angels" is played right before the game begins, while the Jumbotron in the field displays pictures and clips from notable Angels games and their special moments. It starts with Gene Autry back in the sixties, when he owned the first California Angels franchise, and goes through to the most recent Angels events. I see pictures and videos of things that happened when I went to games with Jay, the day the Angels beat the Yankees in the first post season round, Scott Spiezio's game-changing home run, and Darrin Erstadt catching the final out in game seven of the 2002 World Series when the Angels won.

Before the song "Calling All Angels" ends, I've secretly invited a few more angels to the game, those angels I personally know and love.

i Rick Warren, *The Purpose Driven Life* (Philadelphia: Running Press Book Publishers, 2003), p. 94

ii Alice Sebold, *The Lovely Bones* (Boston: Little, Brown and Company, 2002), p. 5

iii Amanda Lamb, *The Evil Next Door* (New York: Berkley Books, 2010), p. 278

iv Jantezen Franklin, *Fasting* (Lake Mary: Charisma House, 2008), p. 11

KAYE BENNETT HAS AN ASSOCIATE's degree in accounting and has been a manager in corporate America for over 30 years. She lives in Riverside, Ca. and attends Crossroads Church in Corona, Ca. where she is known as Miss Kaye.